A Field Guide for
the HR Professional

sales
compensation
essentials

Jerome A. Colletti
Mary S. Fiss
Ted Briggs
S. Scott Sands

About WorldatWork®

WorldatWork is the world's leading not-for-profit professional association dedicated to knowledge leadership in total rewards, compensation, benefits, and work-life. Founded in 1955, WorldatWork focuses on human resources disciplines associated with attracting, retaining and motivating employees. Besides serving as the membership association of the professions, the WorldatWork family of organizations provides education, certification (Certified Compensation Professional — CCP®, Certified Benefits Professional® — CBP, Global Remuneration Professional — GRP® and Work-Life Certified Professional — WLCP™), publications, knowledge resources, surveys, conferences, research and networking. WorldatWork Society of Certified Professionals™; Alliance for Work-Life Progress (AWLP)™ and ITAC, The Telework Advisory Group are part of the WorldatWork family.

WorldatWork Staff Contributors
Publishing Manager: Dan Cafaro
Content Advisor: Kerry Chou, CCP, CBP, GRP
Production Manager: Rebecca Williams Ficker
Graphic Design: Erika Freber

14040 N. Northsight Blvd., Scottsdale, AZ 85260
480/951-9191 Fax 480/483-8352 www.worldatwork.org

TABLE OF CONTENTS

INTRODUCTION

Picture this situation. It involves a brief hallway conversation between Sue Stark, HR manager, and Al Wilson, vice president, worldwide sales, both employees of a major electronic components manufacturing company.

Al Wilson: Hi, Sue. Last week, I participated in Q2 sales reviews with all of our regions. It is now clear to me that we must change our sales compensation plan for next year. We are not achieving the results that we had expected from the changes we made in our sales jobs and the compensation plan we implemented to support our new selling requirements. I am going to call together some folks to address the needs as I see them. I'd like to have the first of what I believe will be several plan-design meetings later this week, probably Friday. Are you available to join us?

Sue Stark: Yes, I would like to participate in that session. What do you see as my role in the meeting and how would you suggest I prepare for it?

Al Wilson: Good questions, Sue. I suggest that you call a couple of our region managers. Ask them to describe to you their experience with the compensation plan. After you have talked with them, get back to me with your thoughts about your role in the meeting and the subsequent work that is required to develop and implement a new plan for next year. Got to run; see you Friday.

In many companies, the situation that confronts Sue Stark is very common. Relatively few sales compensation plans remain the same from one year to the next. This is because companies continually seek to improve their performance with customers. Customers demand effective products, better service and quality, and competitive pricing. The salesforce must deal with changing demands, and in most industries, it's the primary customer contact resource, and therefore, the salesforce is often seen as the "face" of the company. Because of these ongoing changes and the primary importance of the salesforce, company executives must continually examine the effectiveness of sales compensation in motivating and rewarding the salesforce for meeting customer expectations and achieving overall business objectives.

Forty-two percent of the companies that participated in a 2005 survey indicated that HR in their organizations is expected to play a proactive role when a sales leadership team begins to consider a compensation plan change.[1] However, like many HR professionals, Sue has a "part-time" responsibility for sales compensation. It is one of many areas of responsibility that she must be equipped to handle, because her company cannot afford to employ experts in all areas of compensation. There are thousands of professionals like Sue Stark in the HR community who have a need for a field guide like *Sales Compensation Essentials*. HR generalists, compensation professionals and internal change-management consultants often need to quickly understand the basics of sales compensation so they can provide practical guidance to sales executives about the most appropriate process to follow in assessing plan effectiveness, designing a new plan or both. This field guide was written for those individuals as well as all others in a company who are asked to participate in the process of designing and implementing a new sales compensation plan.

How This Book Can Help You

This field guide can meet the varying challenges companies face when they seek to create or revise their sales compensation plans. It has been designed and written so that it can be used in the following ways:

- As a reference guide to the sales compensation concepts, principles and practices that HR professionals need to be aware of as they seek to help their companies achieve business goals and objectives. Thus, it can help you acquire the knowledge and master the use of tools you will need as you help top managers make informed choices about plan design, implementation and ongoing management.

- As a design guide that developers of sales compensation plans can use as they create or modify plans.

- As a change-management guide that various constituencies in a company can use during the sales compensation plan-implementation process.

How This Book Is Organized

This field guide includes nine chapters, which are organized in three sections. The sections correspond to the ways in which most HR professionals are involved with their company's sales compensation plan. Section 1, Contemporary Challenges, sets the stage by discussing the role and involvement of HR professionals in sales compensation, the basic knowledge that they should possess and the skills they should have to help executives identify opportunities for sales improvement through the compensation plan. Chapter 1, The HR Professional's Role in

Sales Compensation, describes the partnering role that HR managers should have with sales leaders when change in the compensation plan is contemplated. Chapter 2, Sales Compensation Fundamentals, explains the basics that are essential to understanding how sales compensation ties into total rewards, the elements of sales compensation and the alternative mechanics to consider in plan design. Chapter 3, Understanding Common Problems in Sales Compensation, identifies the symptoms associated with a failing sales compensation plan. It also describes how a company can successfully address and resolve those problems.

Section 2, Design and Implementation, is the heart of this field guide. It provides you with the principles, tools and techniques needed to design and implement effective sales compensation plans. Chapter 4, Participating in the Design Process, suggests a road map for guiding the process of plan design and implementation. Chapter 5, Assessing Current Plan Effectiveness, explains how to evaluate a current plan in order to identify those features that work effectively and highlight opportunities to improve salesforce productivity through new or revised plan elements. Chapter 6, Designing a New Sales Compensation Plan, describes the business changes and objectives that most commonly influence plan design and the elements of a plan that are most commonly changed.

Section 3, Effective Plan Management, covers three important topics that have a direct impact on the success of a new sales compensation plan. Chapter 7, Implementing a New Plan, explains the requirements of a successful plan launch, including plan documentation, communication, front-line manager training and measuring the effectiveness of a new plan, all of which help top managers determine the level of success they are achieving with its help. Chapter 8, Aligning Other Rewards and Recognition Programs, identifies the most common programs and practices that must align with sales compensation and describes how to ensure that they are complements to the plan and not detractions.

Chapter 9, Governance of Sales Compensation Programs, explains the importance of the governance process, how to determine if governance problems exist and how to develop and implement a governance process that creates an environment for sales compensation plan success.

The principles, tools and techniques we describe in this field guide can help you enhance your knowledge and skills in the field of sales compensation. While authoritative, the guide is not comprehensive in its treatment of the subject.[2] Rather, it boils down to this simple fact: not all HR professionals want to be (or need to be) sales compensation wizards. They have a need to acquire authoritative and practical information about sales compensation in order to address an immediate need with confidence. That is exactly where this field guide comes in handy. It will not turn you into a sales compensation expert, but it definitely will enable you to pick up significant and useful information and immediately apply it. The benefit we hope you gain from this book is the confidence to act competently in situations where you can help sales leaders increase the effectiveness of sales compensation in your company.

---

[1] May, 2005 Colletti-Fiss, LLC Web-based survey

[2] Colt, Stockton B. (Editor) 1998. *The Sales Compensation Handbook*, 2nd Edition, New York: American Management Association

Colletti, Jerome A. and Mary S. Fiss 2001. *Compensating New Sales Roles : How to Design Rewards That Work in Today's Selling Environment*, 2nd Edition, New York : American Management Association

Cichelli, David J. 2003. *Compensating the Sales Force*, New York: McGraw-Hill

chapter I

THE HR PROFESSIONAL'S ROLE IN SALES COMPENSATION

I

The degree of an HR department's involvement with sales compensation plan design and implementation varies from company to company. In some companies, HR's involvement is actively sought by the sales department. In others, its involvement is discouraged or prevented. HR professionals frequently ask, "What can I do to play a more meaningful role in plan design and implementation at my company?" This question is not surprising, because having limited or no involvement in the process of shaping and launching a sales compensation plan means that companies miss the opportunity to use the expertise of their HR staff in key people-management areas. These areas include ensuring that a company's sales compensation plan is designed to attract, retain and reward talented salespeople who can win and keep customers. It is clear that developing and using a compensation plan that helps a company achieve that goal should draw upon the expertise of the HR function. This chapter describes the aspects of sales compensation plan design and implementation in which the HR professional can play a meaningful role. Further, it provides suggestions about actions that a professional can take to perform that role effectively.

Working with the Sales Organization

At many companies, the business partner role defines how HR is expected to work with its assigned organizational client. The client may be either a business unit that includes the sales organization or it may be only the sales organization. When the business partner role is the prevailing model for providing HR services, the HR generalist is faced with a broad range of duties and responsibilities. However, an HR professional's No. 1 priority should be to gain and continually build a thorough understanding of the assigned client's business. When the assigned client is the sales organization, that understanding should include the following:

- Customer markets served and the product/service offerings provided
- Sales channels deployed and the jobs operating within those channels

- Current year's business plan, sales strategies and sales financial goals
- Sales leadership's operational style (e.g., centralized versus decentralized management) as it pertains to various sales management programs – territory assignment, quota allocation, sales crediting – that impact compensation.

Some senior HR professionals have said that an up-to-date understanding of the four areas itemized above is the entry or "ante into the game." As in many business situations, the key to success is the quality of one's relationships with the individuals in senior leadership positions. Relationships built on trust, confidence and respect are acquired over time. HR professionals who have successfully developed effective working relationships with senior sales leaders did so through regular, proactive and meaningful interactions with the sales organization. Figure 1-1 itemizes activities in which an HR/compensation professional should engage to demonstrate a willingness to learn how the sales organization operates. Through these activities, an HR/compensation professional can develop a first-hand understanding of the needs and requirements of the sales organization for compensation support.

FIGURE 1-1 **HR Professional Illustrative Activities – Sales Compensation Plan Involvement**	
Who	**What (Illustrative Interactions)**
• Sales leaders, i.e., top sales executive and regional sales executives (e.g., North America, Europe, Asia/Pacific)	• Regular conversations (monthly, quarterly) about effectiveness of current plans – what's working, what's not; early ideas for change in the future • Participation in sales leadership meetings related to future business planning; implications for sales compensation • Review/discuss with sales leadership teams: quarterly sales results and impact on sales incentive compensation payments, e.g., percent of sales team earning under the plan, percent of sales team achieving target-incentive earnings; overachievement earnings; individual sales performance; and general staffing concerns
• Field sales managers, e.g., first-level sales managers	• Occasional "work withs" to understand challenges faced by field sales managers in their jobs; role sales compensation plays in motivating and managing its sales team • Regular calls to selected field sales managers to gain feedback on current plans – what's working; what's not • Issues/challenges with current plans – what are the most common questions or problems members of the salesforce are experiencing under the plan • Needs relative to managing with the plan, e.g., reports, response to special requests
• Sales staff, e.g., sales operations or adm. executives	• Regular conversations with sales staff supporting the plans to understand employee's perspectives on what's working, what's not and why; early thoughts about opportunities for plan improvement in subsequent year • Periodic meetings to confirm system capabilities, abilities to meet management information needs
• "Sellers," e.g., sales representatives, account managers, sales specialists	• Occasional "ride withs" to understand sales roles and jobs, i.e., how members of the salesforce go about their work, influence they have on customer buying decisions, service work they perform; how sales compensation plan influences their behavior and performance • Periodic salesforce surveys to understand what members of the salesforce like best/least about current plans

Taking the initiative to understand how the sales organization operates assumes that sales leaders are receptive to having HR involved with the sales organization overall, and with the sales compensation plan in particular. Because in some cases this is not a valid assumption, Figure 1-2 indicates some of the more common objections to HR involvement with the plan and provides suggestions for overcoming those objections. These suggestions should be helpful to an HR professional in convincing the top sales executive that his or her involvement with the sales compensation plan will be helpful to both the sales organization and the company.

FIGURE 1-2 **Overcoming Sales Resistance to HR Involvement with Sales Compensation**	
Objections – Sales Executives	**Suggested Response – HR Professional**
• No relevant experience	• Describe experience in sales compensation plan design and design of management incentive plans. • Explain role in the process and key contributions acknowledged by others. • Describe seminars or courses taken in sales compensation.
• No understanding of our sales channels, process, jobs	• Ask for the opportunity to develop that understanding by visiting field locations, doing "work withs" with field managers and going on calls with sales reps.
• No time	• Explain that priorities have been adjusted to make time available to work on sales compensation.
• Don't know where it would make sense to involve you	• Suggest a process; offer ideas about specific tasks that HR could undertake and complete; and describe outcomes and benefits.

Whether HR is considered an internal consultant or a policy gatekeeper, involvement of the HR professional with the sales compensation plan is important to business success. Meaningful involvement is most likely to take place in situations where the professional has developed a thorough understanding of how sales operates and has built an effective working relationship with key sales leaders throughout the sales organization. Additionally, HR/compensation professionals must develop and improve upon their knowledge of sales compensation principles, practices and techniques. Every HR/compensation professional with responsibility for sales compensation should ask, "What am I doing to continually improve my mastery of the tools and techniques required to provide innovative compensation solutions to the sales challenges faced by my company?"

This book's overall goal is to provide you with the tools and knowledge required to support the sales organization through compensation solutions. In particular, the goal of this chapter is to describe some of the competencies that require mastery in today's business environment. These competencies include the following:

- Knowing how to help sales executives address and resolve sales compensation problems as they arise during the course of a year
- Knowing how to assess the effectiveness of the sales compensation plan and therefore how and when to help sales executives make plan changes in order to increase sales effectiveness through compensation
- Having the ability to lead or participate in a design process that includes advising management on which jobs should be eligible to participate in the sales compensation plan, the appropriate level of pay for those jobs, what type of plan is appropriate and how the incentive arrangement should be structured
- Developing a holistic understanding of the company's sales management programs and the role their interdependence plays in the company's achievement of its sales goals
- Understanding how communication strategies and tactics are created and executed in order to ensure that a new or changed plan produces the expected business results.

Six Areas of Sales Compensation Plan Involvement

A solid understanding of how the sales organization operates and the respect of sales leadership are important prerequisites for gaining involvement with the sales compensation plan. Once those prerequisites are established, it is equally important to be confident about where and how HR involvement with sales compensation is beneficial to a company and its salesforce. The remainder of this chapter will describe the following six areas in which HR involvement is most often desired and/or needed:

1. Problem Resolution

Many HR professionals indicate that their first significant involvement with the sales compensation plan was the result of a major problem that sales leaders believed was caused by the plan. This can often occur in companies in which HR's involvement with sales compensation is either a new or emerging responsibility. In such a company, an HR professional might be invited to help address a problem with the plan because there is a new awareness among sales executives that HR can bring an objective perspective and fresh thinking that could help address and resolve the problem. This, of course, means that the HR professional must have the knowledge, skills and experience to make a meaningful contribution to a solution. HR professionals are too frequently not asked for their involvement because they are seen as not having adequate experience and skills in sales compensation. They are further perceived as not possessing a sufficiently intimate knowledge of the business to be of help to the sales organization. The old adage of "...be prepared..." is quite relevant here. An HR professional must possess applicable knowledge, skill and experience in order to make a value-added contribution.

Common examples of plan problems that HR professionals are frequently asked to investigate include the following: 1) Sales employee dissatisfaction with the plan; 2) Exceptions to either payout calculations or plan rules; 3) Overpayments or underpayments; and 4) Turnover either higher or lower than internally expected, industry benchmarks or both. Seasoned HR professionals should be equipped to help the sales organization address problems such as these.

Most experienced HR professionals understand human motivation and how to tap into the workforce through interviews and surveys in order to determine root causes of job dissatisfaction. Many HR professionals have also acquired analytical skills that can be applied to determining the turnover rate and its relationship to overall industry conditions. The important point is this: Because the problems just mentioned are common sales compensation problems, a thoughtful HR professional should be able to respond with a plan of action when called on for help by the sales organization. This book is one source of information that can help develop that action plan.

Generally speaking, the exact cause of the perceived sales compensation problem is less important than how one goes about helping sales leaders address and fix the problem. Two hallmarks of success in resolving such problems, at least from the sales function's perspective, are a willingness on the part of HR to act swiftly and authoritatively to identify the root causes of the problem and the ability to help sales leaders formulate practical alternative solutions that can be implemented quickly. It is worth mentioning, however, that HR should take great care in identifying and isolating the root cause of the problems associated with sales compensation. In a majority of cases in which sales compensation is blamed for shortcomings in its overall effectiveness, the problem's root cause actually lies elsewhere.

Consider this common situation. When members of the salesforce are not earning their incentive compensation opportunity under the plan, field sales managers may report that their people are dissatisfied with the plan. However, the dissatisfaction may have little to do with either the incentive opportunity or the payout formula mechanics. The real problem may well be overly ambitious sales growth targets reflected in sales quotas that may be unachievable by a disproportionately high percentage of the salesforce. The important point here is this: It is easy to attach blame to the sales compensation plan, but rarely will a fix to the sales compensation plan solve a performance problem that has its root cause elsewhere. In Chapter 3, you will learn more about problems that are common to sales compensation plans regardless of industry or company and how the HR professional can help sales leaders address and resolve them.

2. Design and Implementation Process

Companies are increasingly following a documented process for the design and implementation of their sales compensation plans. Most processes include the following four major activities:

a. Assessment: How effective is the current sales compensation plan? What evidence is there to suggest that the plan may require modification or may need to be replaced by a completely new plan, for example, change in business strategy; implementation of new or restructured sales channels, jobs or both; new product launch?

b. Design and testing: What changes could be made to incentive pay mechanics? (That is, linking performance to pay.) And, will such change redirect sales behavior in the areas management requires for achievement of the coming year's business results? Can such changes be supported with sales financial data (i.e., costing and individual performance modeling) that show a proposed change will result in a material improvement in business results?

c. Implementation: How will plan changes or a completely new plan be introduced to the salesforce so that it will produce maximum motivational mileage and thus contribute to achievement of desired business results?

d. Monitoring: What actions are taken to confirm that the salesforce has received and understands the plans and field sales managers are managing effectively with the new plans?

It is easier to lay out these activities than to actually execute them effectively. There are three common flaws in the plan design and implementation process that you should watch out for at your company.

a. The first type of flaws are those that are present both in the underlying process used to assess the current plan and in the process to either design new plans or modify current plans. There are three common process errors: (i) Executing design tasks out of sequence (e.g., modifying the incentive formula without first assessing how well the current plan is working, understanding what the new business objectives may be or both); (ii) Limiting design work to a single function such as sales, when the design process would actually benefit from a multifunctional approach that includes sales, finance, HR and others; and, (iii) Misunderstanding how long the design process takes and thus either spending too little time (the most common mistake) or too much time on it.

It is frequently the HR professional's role to ensure that one or more of these three process flaws does not encumber the design process. To do so, HR (or the designated process owner) should pull together representatives from all of the functions that currently have involvement with the plan and agree on the safeguards that will be put into the process – for example, agreeing to a defined project work plan with regular checkpoint meetings – to ensure that none of these flaws will be allowed to creep into the design process.

b. Design errors are the second most common category of flaws that occur during the process. Common errors include a salary/incentive ratio that is inappropriate for a particular sales job; leverage (i.e., upside incentive opportunity) that is either too little or too high; performance measures that cannot be influenced or accurately tracked and credited to members of the salesforce; and sales quotas (goals) that do not appropriately reflect the sales potential in salesforce territories. Here, too, the HR professional should take an active role in confirming with others who are involved with the sales compensation plan that these types of design flaws are common and should be avoided in the process.

c. Ineffective implementation and ineffective monitoring of performance represent the third set of common flaws that occur when changes are made to a sales compensation plan. Examples of ineffective implementation include no formal process for communicating plan change, no defined/assigned change accountabilities and lack of a clear leadership message about change (what will change, why change is important now, and how change will benefit customers, salespeople and the company). Examples of ineffective monitoring of the new plan's impact on the business include no predefined measures of plan success; no set time period (e.g., after first payout, after first quarter, midyear) for assessing success; and no reports provided to field sales managers so they can see how the salesforce is performing under the plan.

HR typically plays an important role in developing materials for communicating the compensation plan to the salesforce. Employee communications is a key competency of many HR professionals. This is therefore one area where help is usually welcomed. However, HR generally plays a less active role in monitoring the effectiveness of new sales compensation plans. This should not be the case. Because the plan can play an important role in salesforce performance management, the HR professional should be proactive in helping sales leaders define how success under the new (or revised) plan will be assessed and measured.

3. Sales Compensation Guiding Principles

Guiding principles are the main values that best-practice companies follow in order to design effective and successful sales compensation plans. These principles are based on and support the company's philosophy of pay. However, they are rarely documented and assembled in one place for ready reference and use. There are two disadvantages to not using a set of documented guiding principles during a plan-design process:

  a. The absence of guiding principles is analogous to trying to shoot at a target in the dark. How do you know when you have hit the bull's-eye? The answer, of course, is that you don't know. Thus, guiding principles set forth the standards against which a plan or plans are designed. The principles provide each of the participants in the plan design process with the same understanding of what the design team is shooting for at a conceptual level and in terms of the design results. A statement of sales compensation guiding principles typically includes the following topics: 1) business strategy; 2) competitive compensation positioning; 3) plan types; 4) performance management; and 5) administrative considerations, such as a desire for plan simplicity, management commitment to effective communication.

  b. The second disadvantage of not having and using guiding principles is that it is virtually impossible to know the extent to which a new plan has contributed to business success. For example, the statement of guiding principles typically defines the expected performance distribution under the sales compensation plan. Without the benefit of a specific expectation in this area, it is difficult to determine if the plan paid more or fewer salespeople than expected.

You will learn more about guiding principles in Chapter 2. However, it is sufficient to say at this point that an HR professional involved with a sales compensation plan should encourage the design team to formulate and use a set of guiding principles for the plan-design and implementation process. Using guiding principles will provide the design team with a blueprint that both sets forth clear direction and can save time during the process itself.

4. Competitive Pay Assessments

In most companies, sales executives look to the compensation plan to help attract and retain the caliber of people they need to successfully sell to and interact with customers. Because attracting and retaining top-notch talent is one of the most persistent challenges faced by sales organizations, HR has an opportunity to make a major contribution to the sales compensation plan through competitive pay assessment. HR's role is to assure sales executives that pay levels are externally competitive and internally equitable (or otherwise consistent with the organization's compensation objectives based on the roles and responsibilities of the jobs).

It is typically HR's job to assemble labor-market data that can be used in making decisions about where to set sales pay levels. This means that HR is responsible for identifying and selecting reliable labor-market surveys for use in job pricing. A company will usually rely on two to four survey sources for competitive data. It is commonly an HR professional who has been given the responsibility to select and purchase the survey data and to assist with or manage the data submission from the company. More information about this process is provided in Chapter 5.

HR should help management determine the appropriate competitive position (e.g., median, 75th percentile) in the labor market for use in pricing a company's particular sales jobs. This is an important contribution to the sales compensation plan because the total cash compensation level for each sales job must be large enough to attract, motivate and retain top-notch talent, as well as pay for the performance that drives desired business results.

5. Industry Trends and Practices

Sales executives are vitally interested in how various practices affecting the sales compensation plan compare to others in their industry. The HR professional, through participation in industry networking groups and compensation survey job-matching sessions, can be in an excellent position to gain an understanding of trends and practices that may affect the sales compensation plan. Thus, the HR professional should be a member of and active participant in industry and survey groups.

Sales leaders are also typically interested in knowing about changes taking place in sales channels and sales coverage in the markets in which they compete for customers. Job-matching sessions in industry-survey groups are often one place to learn about how others in the industry are covering the market. For example, if new jobs that your company does not have are surfacing in either the surveys or the job-matching sessions, that may be an indication of a trend in sales coverage that should be brought to the attention of sales leadership.

A third area of interest to sales leaders is how the operation of the sales compensation plan is affected by administrative practices. For example, draws, sales crediting and splits (duplicate crediting) are all topics of great importance to sales leaders as they consider a current plan's effectiveness. An HR professional involved with sales compensation should consistently make every effort to learn about industry trends and practices that are likely to impact both the thinking about and the planning for sales compensation, and share those findings with sales leaders. Doing so increases the value that the HR professional provides to the sales organization.

6. Plan Effectiveness Assessment

At most companies, sales compensation Return On Investment (ROI) is an important topic. In fact, a recent WorldatWork survey reports that 86 percent of the respondents indicated that how to determine sales compensation plan ROI is a top priority at their company.[1] The reason for this interest is that companies have begun to think of sales compensation as an investment in improving overall sales effectiveness instead of thinking about it as an expense to be minimized. Thus, they have shifted their outlook and view sales compensation as a means of achieving increased volume and quality of sales. This shift in thinking provides an opportunity for the HR professional to help sales leaders rethink their approach to plan assessment.

One of the reasons for the difficulty of assessing plan effectiveness is the existence of unclear expectations for sales compensation. The best time to gain an understanding of what sales leaders expect to accomplish through the compensation plan is at the time the plan is being formulated. The key question is: What are the outcomes that sales executives (and, in turn, top management) anticipate from a new plan? These outcomes are the quantifiable results that management wishes to derive from its investment in cash compensation for the salesforce.

The selection of assessment metrics, including ROI, is determined by the goals of the business and the priorities set for the sales organization by top management. Thus, the actual metrics used are situational; that is, they should be tailored to a company's particular situation and set at the beginning of the new sales compensation plan year. Because the optimal environment is one in which the HR professional is a very active participant in the assessment of a current sales compensation plan's effectiveness, two subsequent chapters (Chapters 5 and 7) provide information and tools to help with that work.

Summing Up

Sales compensation is one of the more important tools that a company uses to attract, retain and reward talented members of the salesforce. Involvement with the sales compensation plan offers an opportunity for an HR professional to make important contributions to business success. To gain involvement with the plan requires that an HR professional have the respect and confidence of sales leaders and other key executives (e.g., finance, marketing, IT) who have had a role in determining the plan in the past. Gaining that respect and confidence will require an HR professional to demonstrate an understanding of the company's

---

[1] Jerome A. Colletti and Stockton Colt, "Identifying a Complex Sales Environment: Results of a Special Member Survey," *workspan*, April 2004

business – markets, products, current sales model, competitors – and to possess the competencies associated with sound plan design and implementation. This means that the HR professional must develop and demonstrate the expertise to work with sales leaders and others involved with the sales compensation plan.

HR professionals should be proactive in seeking opportunities to become involved with the sales compensation plan. There are six areas in which the involvement can be both professionally meaningful and materially beneficial to the company. Those areas include problem resolution, design and implementation process, sales compensation guiding principles, competitive pay assessment, industry trends and practices, and plan-effectiveness assessment. An HR professional involved with a sales compensation plan should continually strive to improve mastery of the concepts, tools and techniques required to provide innovative, yet practical, solutions to effectively paying the salesforce for desired results.

chapter 2

SALES COMPENSATION
FUNDAMENTALS

Learning about sales compensation can be like learning a new language, a language that has its own unique key concepts and terms. One of the most difficult challenges of working on sales compensation within your organization is ensuring that everyone is using the same language. The following sections in this chapter describe fundamental concepts that are widely used in discussions about sales compensation:

- Compensation Tied to Total Rewards
- Variable Pay Plan Categories
- Sales Compensation Philosophy
- Guiding Principles
- Timing Considerations
- Alternative Mechanics.

Your knowledge of the fundamental concepts of the language of sales compensation will add to your ability to effectively participate in your organization's sales compensation plan design and implementation.

Compensation Tied to Total Rewards

It is important to first understand the charter and scope of sales compensation. The amount of pay called "sales compensation" typically cannot fulfill all of the attraction, motivation and retention requirements of a total rewards strategy by itself. In fact, most companies suffer from using sales results and sales compensation earnings as the only indicators of a sales professional's performance. Many companies fall into the trap of overemphasizing the pay results to the point that sellers say, "If it's not in the sales compensation plan, then I'm not paid for it." While no one can argue that these factors do not matter, other results are also important, and may not be built into the sales compensation plan or performance management evaluation. This fact becomes even more important when your company asks talented sales professionals to tackle more challenging sales assignments or when your sales organization is integrated into a merged or restructured organization. An important responsibility of the HR professional is to help the company learn to accept and communicate that "total compensation," including all of the aspects of the rewards of work, is used to reward "total performance."

WorldatWork defines total rewards as "All of the tools available to the employer that may be used to attract, retain and motivate employees. Total rewards include everything the employee perceives to be of value resulting from the employment relationship." *The Rewards of Work* study[1] describes the five types of rewards shown in Figure 2-1. As you work with the sales organization, it is important to have a common understanding of what is included in all the reward types as they pertain to a salesforce. This common understanding will help ensure that all components of the total rewards system are appropriately aligned with the company's expectations for sales jobs.

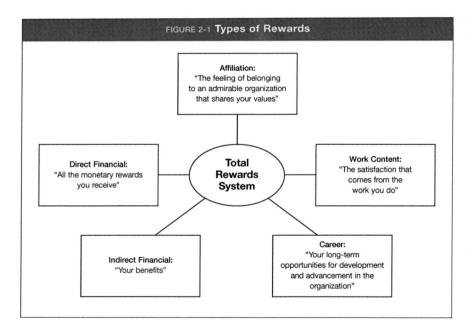

FIGURE 2-1 **Types of Rewards**

Affiliation:
"The feeling of belonging to an admirable organization that shares your values"

Direct Financial:
"All the monetary rewards you receive"

Total Rewards System

Work Content:
"The satisfaction that comes from the work you do"

Indirect Financial:
"Your benefits"

Career:
"Your long-term opportunities for development and advancement in the organization"

---

[1] Paul W. Mulvey, Gerald E. Ledford, Jr. and Peter V. LeBlanc. (Third Quarter, 2000.) "Rewards of Work: How They Drive Performance, Retention and Satisfaction." WorldatWork Journal.

Direct and Indirect Financials (Total Pay). In some companies, a significant amount of time and energy is devoted to determining the total pay plan for the salesforce. Elements of total pay include the following:

- Base salary
- Incentive compensation – bonus, commission
- Specialized Performance Incentives for Field Force (SPIFFs), including sales contests
- Recognition/Overachievers Club
- Benefits
- Perquisites.

While total pay is very important in attracting, motivating, rewarding and retaining a highly effective salesforce, putting too much attention on it could create a culture that is counter to business success. Sales leaders in high-performing sales organizations increasingly seek to strike the right balance between total pay and other types of rewards.

Affiliation. It is critical for most employees to belong to an admirable organization. All employees are interested in the company's vision and strategy. For the salesforce, however, such interest is particularly strong because its members "face" company customers regularly. Thus, the following elements of "affiliation" are particularly important:

- Business vision and aspirations
- Company image, reputation; for example, how customers feel about the company
- Top management's support and recognition of the salesforce
- Consistent sales-performance management activities
- Support and mutual respect of peers
- Openness of communication
- Ethics – commitment to doing business honestly.

Affiliation can have a significant impact for sales organizations if many sellers are remote or home-based employees. Extra efforts may be required to ensure they remain advocates of the company rather than solely advocates of customers to whom they are closest.

Career. Most sales employees welcome the opportunity to grow in their career, although many find a role as an individual contributor highly satisfying. For the salesforce, key elements of individual and career growth include the following:

- Performance management and coaching style

- Opportunities for career advancement within sales and other areas of the company (e.g., sales operations or product development and marketing)
- Opportunities for individual development and growth.

Work Content. Finally, the quality and content of the job is now more important than ever. With that in mind, sales employees at all levels have heightened interest in the quality of the job and the workplace. Key elements of that building block include the following:

- Meaningful involvement of first-line sales management
- Working relationships (trust and commitment) with colleagues in other functions
- Effectiveness and efficiency of the selling process
- Effective sales-support tools (e.g., CRM, mobile computing, quote/configuration automation) and resources
- Innovation and commitment to new products
- Investment in training – market, products and selling skills.

You probably hear most often that the sales compensation plan is the "most important tool" the company possesses for the purpose of attracting, retaining and motivating its salesforce. However, work content and other "intangibles" are often more influential than pay, especially for those in complex selling roles. Understanding how the sales compensation plan fits into total rewards at your company is a key element in working to develop a philosophy and guidelines for the program. While all five areas of the total rewards model are important, most companies fail to excel in all. In advising your company, you should evaluate which areas provide the best competitive differentiation for your current and prospective talent pool and place strong emphasis in those areas.

Variable Pay Plan Categories

Before addressing the details of plan-design elements, it is important to understand that there are three basic variable pay or rewards plan categories in which customer-facing employees might participate: individual, team and corporate. As you will learn in later chapters, these categories might be short-term or long-term, and can use cash or non-cash as the reward. The right type of incentives must be aligned with each role to ensure an effective total rewards strategy. Appropriate incentives balance the degree of salesperson impact and the company's ability to measure that impact so that the program or plan is fair, equitable and manageable.

Individual incentives create payouts based on the results of an individual relative to his or her assignment. While there may be team members (on the account team, for example) sharing in those results, the individual's pay is based solely or primarily on what that person's accounts or territories achieve. Companies typically use this kind of plan for individual contributors (sales reps, account managers, product specialists) as well as sales management.

Team incentives are based on how a group of similarly functioned or similarly tasked people performs collectively. The plan combines all results, and the members of the team receive payment on the total result. Although on occasion there is some modification at the individual level, the team results drive the payouts. This kind of plan best fits pooled resources assigned to support a range of sellers, in which individuals do not always have direct control over the specific assignments or opportunities to which they are assigned and may work across multiple opportunities.

Corporate incentives represent broader plans based on total company or division performance. This typically occurs through some funding process that may or may not allow for differentiation at the individual level. Companies typically implement this kind of plan for a variety of roles beyond customer-facing jobs. This may include sales support functions that have minimal customer contact, support a wide range of sales professionals or have many other duties outside of sales support.

"Sales compensation" generally describes individual or team incentives, or a combination of both. Rewards are shorter-term (the measurement period is typically one year or less) and the reward currency is cash.

Sales Compensation Philosophy

To develop an effective sales compensation program, the design should be consistent with your company's compensation philosophy. This philosophy is frequently both undocumented and informal. It is therefore very helpful to confirm and document the philosophy in order to support alignment across all related programs. Elements of the framework for a sales compensation philosophy are as follows:

1. **Objectives:** Confirmation of the strategic foundation of the programs
   - Legal and regulatory requirements
   - Business and financial alignment
   - Personnel objectives.

2. **Labor Market Comparison:** Appropriate companies and jobs

3. **Competitive Positioning:** Percentile positioning and relationship to other jobs in the company based on the skills, competencies and focus required to successfully perform in each role

4. **Salary/Variable Pay Ratio Factors:** Based on the company's philosophy of risk vs. reward

5. **Base Salary Determination:** Elements/programs that will be used

6. **Short-Term and Long-Term Incentives:** Eligibility/type.

Guiding Principles

Once the sales compensation philosophy is defined and documented, various "guiding principles" related to plan design can be determined. These principles are based on key elements of the philosophy. They can be used throughout the organization to "test" decisions as sales compensation plans are developed or revised in order to ensure that the plans are consistent with the company's philosophy. Examples of "guiding principles" are provided in Figure 2-2.

Once the conceptual groundwork has been established, it's important to understand the criteria for determining who should participate in the sales compensation plan and the key components of any sales compensation plan framework: target earnings, the mix of fixed and variable pay, upside earnings potential, performance measures and performance standards.

FIGURE 2-2 Illustrative "Guiding Principles"

- Plans are aligned with the company's business strategy and primary goals – sales growth, profitability, new product sales and other strategic initiatives (as highlighted in the business plan).

- Plans are designed to the specific accountabilities of each job.

- Plans differentiate various levels of performance.

- The absolute number of performance measures is limited (i.e., up to three) within a specific plan, and the capability to track and report results is confirmed prior to plan finalization.

- The goals of the salesforce are based on optimal performance distribution. This means that threshold and excellence performance levels are realistically achievable; that is, they will be set so that at least 90 percent of the salesforce achieves threshold, 60 percent – 70 percent achieves/exceeds quota and 10 percent – 15 percent achieves/exceeds excellence.

- The company is committed to using plans that are simple, flexible and self-calculating by plan participants. Approved plans are ones that can be administered in a timely and cost-efficient manner, with minimal requirements for manual intervention.

- Management at all levels of the organization is committed to clearly communicating the plans and to providing the support required to enable the salesforce to succeed under the compensation plan.

Eligibility for Sales Compensation

When your company is going through a change initiative, and the result is new jobs, new products or new processes, it is critical to validate the eligibility of relevant jobs for participation in the sales compensation plan. Whether the job is direct-to-consumer (like a retail clerk), or business-to-business, the key criterion is the role each job plays in the sales process, particularly the degree to which the job is involved in persuading a customer to buy the company's products or services. To validate the eligibility of relevant jobs for participation in the sales compensation plan, the team must understand the sales process (whether it has been formally documented or can be defined specifically based on case example), from developing and qualifying leads to persuading the customer to buy, and then fulfilling the order.

In recent years, there has been an increasing tendency to make more service- and fulfillment-related jobs eligible for sales incentive pay. However, one key differential between sales incentive pay and other variable pay is the degree to which target incentive pay is included in the calculation for market-rate competitive pay. For many jobs, the base wage, or base salary, is considered 100 percent of the target pay for that position, and incentive earnings are added on. As the HR expert on the team, your job may include the need to challenge eligibility assumptions in order to ensure that jobs are treated equitably, consistent with market/industry practice and generally accepted principles of compensation plan design. Three primary criteria for eligibility to be on either individual or team sales plans are as follows:

1. The primary responsibility of employees in designated sales jobs is customer contact and persuading the customer to do business with the company.

2. Employees can affect sales results and may have assigned sales goals.

3. Sales results can be tracked and accurately measured at the employee level.

Target Earnings

Three key compensation terms used in sales compensation are defined in Figure 2-3 on page 30. The target cash compensation (TCC) for a job includes the base pay that is available for "expected" or "acceptable" performance (either a fixed base salary for the job or the midpoint of the job's salary range) plus the at-risk pay available for achieving expected results (e.g., the quota). As you work with the sales organization, it is important to remember that TCC is a broadly accepted term, but specific industries may use different terms to describe it. Other names used for TCC include the high-technology term on-target earnings (OTE) and total target compensation (TTC), which is frequently used in the services industry.

FIGURE 2-3 Key Sales Compensation Terms and Definitions

- Target Cash Compensation (TCC): TCC is the total cash compensation (including base salary and incentive compensation) available for achieving expected results.

- Salary/Incentive Mix: Salary/incentive mix is the relationship between the base salary and the planned (or target) incentive amounts in the total cash compensation package at planned or expected performance. The two portions of the mix, expressed as percentages, always equal 100 percent. For example, an 80/20 mix means that 80 percent of the TCC is base salary and 20 percent is incentive pay at target performance.

- Leverage: Leverage is the amount of increased or upside incentive opportunity – in addition to target incentive pay – that management expects outstanding performers to earn. Leverage may be expressed as a ratio of upside to target (e.g., 2:1), a multiple of the target incentive (e.g., 2 times target) or as a total of the target incentive opportunity plus the multiple of target at upside (e.g., triple leverage).

Possibly the single most critical factor to use in determining the appropriate TCC for a job is confirmation of that job's role, not simply the title given to that job in your company. Titles vary significantly from company to company, but the job role (e.g., telesales, counter sales, geographic sales, technical specialist) is the designator used to match your company's job to externally available data about how companies pay jobs having the same role.

The process of confirming the TCC for a sales job is essentially the same process used to benchmark other jobs in your company: Once the job has been confirmed, both external market data and internal structure and equity are used to establish the parameters of the job value. The *Survey Handbook & Directory* (to be updated by WorldatWork in 2006), as well as booklets in the WorldatWork *How-to Series for the HR Professional*, provides a helpful set of tutorials and summaries on how to obtain and use market data. See Figure 2-4 for a brief summary of several factors you, or the person on your team charged with market pay determination, should consider. Some specific analyses for consideration of market pay positioning are provided in Chapter 5.

FIGURE 2-4 Using Survey Results

- Have at least two survey sources for key jobs.
- Ensure the competition is represented (in the participant list).
- Verify job matches with the published descriptions (work with sales management to ensure matches are accurate).
- Based on the company's pay philosophy, decide on the statistics to be extracted (e.g., 50th or 75th percentile, median, weighted average).
- Extract data for each compensation level and productivity analysis (base salary, incentive pay, target cash compensation, quota).
- Use discrete data points instead of using averages or blending different data sources for sales compensation surveys. Participants and job matches differ, as does quality of data.
- Synchronize the survey data with economic data (events in the marketplace and the economy).

Source: *2003-2004 Survey Handbook & Directory* (WorldatWork, 2002)

The results of the competitive/market analysis will need to be balanced against your own internal compensation structure and programs as well as equity requirements across similar job levels in different functions. This can be done on either a "base pay plus" or "total cash compensation" basis, but is generally required to ensure internal equity and consistency with legal requirements. It is also a tool that is helpful during the dreaded "FLSA audit" that you or someone in HR is typically responsible for periodically completing. It is sometimes quite a challenge to confirm or determine the appropriate FLSA status for sales jobs, both inside and outside; however, this should always be done in light of the actual requirements of the job rather than a perceived lack of internal standing if job status changes.

Salary/Incentive Ratio and Target Upside

Sellers are willing to accept putting a degree of their pay at risk if there is significant upside pay available for achieving or exceeding expectations or average productivity. Several behavioral theories underlie the concept of "risk and reward:"

- **Achievement Need:** D.C. McClelland defines achievement need as the desire to perform in terms of a standard of excellence or as a desire to be successful in competitive situations.

- **Reinforcement Theory:** As demonstrated through many studies, most notably those of B.F. Skinner, the frequency of a behavior is likely to be increased when a valuable reward is directly linked to that behavior.

- **Expectancy Theory:** This theory of employee motivation suggests that the salesforce makes decisions based on the degree of perceived attractiveness of the outcome.

These theories come into play for two important aspects of sales compensation plan design: incentive mix and upside opportunity (leverage). Setting them correctly is important to a successful process.

Salary/Incentive Ratio (Mix)

While the target cash compensation (TCC) for a job is, of course, very important to the job incumbents, *salary/incentive mix* has at least equal importance because it directly impacts take-home pay and cash flow. Incentive mix is typically expressed as a ratio (e.g., 50/50 or 70/30) in which the first number represents the percentage of target pay in base salary and the second number represents the percentage of target pay at risk for achieving expectations or target performance. Some companies describe mix by stating variable incentive as a percentage of base. While this is a fairly simple mathematical calculation, it does not visibly express the concept of at-risk pay as an element of the total cash opportunity.

Since mix indicates the proportion of pay at risk, a job with an aggressive mix (50 percent or more of the TCC is incentive pay) has less predictable cash flow, while a job with a less aggressive mix (e.g., with 25 percent or less of the TCC as incentive) has a much more predictable cash flow associated with it. Many of the same factors that were used to help you determine the most appropriate TCC for each job also apply as you consider the right mix of base pay and at-risk or incentive pay as well as the amount of upside (or above-target incentive pay) that should be available. Figure 2-5 provides an illustration of mix.

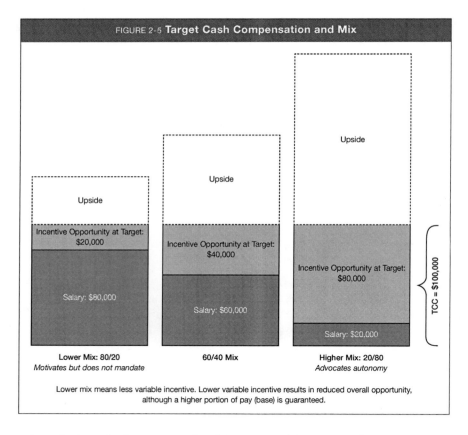

FIGURE 2-5 **Target Cash Compensation and Mix**

Lower mix means less variable incentive. Lower variable incentive results in reduced overall opportunity, although a higher portion of pay (base) is guaranteed.

Several job- and sales process-related factors, in addition to market-practice data, should be used to determine the proportion of pay that is base and the proportion that is incentive pay, as shown Figure 2-6 on page 33.

FIGURE 2-6 **Factors That Impact Salary/Incentive Mix**

Sales Process	Role in the Process	Type of Product or Service
– Transactional (more pay at risk)	– Team member	– Commodity
– Consultative (less pay at risk)	(less pay at risk)	(more pay at risk)
– Product-focused	– Key impact on decision to buy	– Specialty or custom
(more pay at risk)	(more pay at risk)	(less pay at risk)
– Relationship-focused	– Provides leads/access	– Sold on price
(less pay at risk))	or fulfillment only	(more pay at risk)
– Many, frequent sales	(less pay at risk)	– Sold on value
(more pay at risk)	– Provides key expertise in	(less pay at risk)
– Few, large sales	product, customers or segments	
(less pay at risk)	(less pay at risk)	
– Long sales cycle	– Limited expertise required	
(less pay at risk)	for sales success	
	(more pay at risk)	

The most critical element is the role of the seller. The incentive mix should reflect the degree of influence the sales professional has over the purchase decision and the value of that transaction. The more important and influential the seller, the higher the mix (higher percentage put into variable compensation).

Industry surveys indicate that the overall market-average mix for sales positions is 70/30. Therefore, a job with a 50/50 mix or less implies that the role places significantly more emphasis on the selling skills and influence of the seller as factors that cause the customer to buy. A 90/10 mix would imply that the salesperson is only one of many factors affecting the customer's buying decision or the absolute volume purchased.

Based on the factors shown in Figure 2-6, establishing or confirming the mix applied to the TCC for each job requires an accurate and current definition of the position. While input from sales and other functions is useful to confirm roles and processes, as the HR professional on the team, this task is likely to be your responsibility as well.

One final consideration for mix is how it is expressed and the effect of that on a merit pay increase. While mix is the proportion of base vs. variable pay as proportions of 100, there are several ways to implement the concept. (See Figure 2-7 on page 34.)

How mix is expressed for your sales organization has direct effects on the way a merit increase is handled. As discussed previously, merit pay is a useful financial tool for rewarding total performance; however, merit pay increases may also have unforeseen consequences. If these increases are used with your sales organization, it is important to add dollars to salary while ensuring that this change does not dilute the importance of the variable component of the sales compensation plan. Therefore, increased dollars should be spread across both base and incentive at the desired ratio to ensure the intensity of focus on the sales results desired.

	Description of Components		Illustration
Method	**Salary**	**Incentive**	**($100,000 and 50/50 mix)**
Uniform Base/Uniform Incentive: Mix is actual and uniform for all job incumbents	Uniform salary for all incumbents in the same job	Uniform incentive opportunity as a discrete dollar amount for all incumbents in the same job	$50,000 base + $50,000 incentive
Base Range/Uniform Incentive: Mix varies by individual; less aggressive (less pay at risk as a percent of the total) for those higher in the range	Salary range is implemented consistent with practice in other functions; salary midpoint used to determine mix	Uniform incentive opportunity as a discrete dollar amount for all incumbents in the same job	$40,000 – $60,000 base range, $50,0000 midpoint + $50,000 incentive
Salary Plus Percentage of Salary: Mix is actual and uniform for all job incumbents	Salary range is implemented consistent with practice in other functions	Incentive opportunity as the same percent of the individual's salary for each incumbent in the same job	$50,0000 base + 100% of base incentive

FIGURE 2-7 **Implementing Mix**

Target Upside (Leverage)

Once the value of the incentive opportunity has been established or verified, that is, the TCC and the mix have been confirmed, the leverage (the amount of upside pay earned at some defined level of performance above 100 percent) needs to be determined. Mix and leverage are strongly linked in the minds of most sales compensation plan participants. The reason is fairly simple – the more pay there is at risk, the greater the upside opportunity. An important note: The definition of "leverage" does *not* necessarily mean that a plan is "capped" (i.e., that earnings are limited). However, determination of the additional pay available at levels of performance above expected performance will help immensely when it comes time to design the formulas in the plan.

While upside affects all individuals who overachieve target expectations, the upside/leverage ratio reflects the opportunity available for your sales organization's top performers (typically the top 5 percent to 10 percent of your salesforce on a job-by-job basis). The amount of upside available is based on the role of the sales position, the ability to overachieve and financial affordability. For example, sales teams, account managers with very large quotas and senior sales managers have little opportunity to significantly overachieve their target numbers. In these situations, the upside ratios tend to be lower, which puts more pressure on setting more aggressive target compensation levels for meeting expectations. Figure 2-8 on page 35 provides an overview of the relationships of role to the upside/leverage ratio across industries.

There are several ways to express leverage: as a ratio of upside to target (e.g., 2:1), as a multiple of target (e.g., 2 times target) or as a total of the target incentive opportunity plus the multiple of target at upside (e.g., triple leverage).

- Direct Seller Territory- Highest
- Account Manager – Many Accounts – Highest
- Account Manager – Single/Few Accounts – High
- Outbound Telesales – High
- Inbound Telesales – Medium to low, based on job focus
- Channel Account Manager-Medium
- Overlay Sales Specialists – Medium
- First-Line Sales Management – Medium
- Second-Line and Above Sales Management – Low

The term you should use is the one that has been used in your company in the past – the one that your team finds easiest to use and to explain to others. Figure 2-9 illustrates leverage and how each term could be used to describe the same upside opportunity.

Figure 2-10 on page 36 shows the impact of a change in leverage on total upside opportunity.

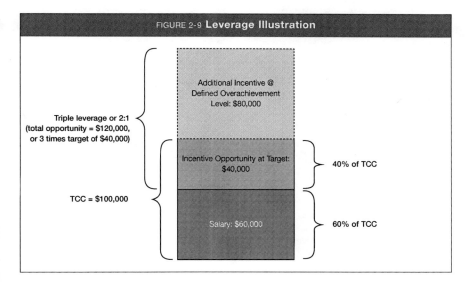

FIGURE 2-9 **Leverage Illustration**

Additional Incentive @ Defined Overachievement Level: $80,000

Triple leverage or 2:1 (total opportunity = $120,000, or 3 times target of $40,000)

Incentive Opportunity at Target: $40,000 — 40% of TCC

TCC = $100,000

Salary: $60,000 — 60% of TCC

Plan Measures and Performance Standards

Once the percentage or amount of variable compensation and upside are determined, your company must then select the most financially and strategically important measures for which to pay these dollars, as well as the range of performance used in calculating payout.

Performance Measures

The following factors are used when deciding on the most appropriate performance measures:

- Job: Measures should reflect job accountabilities, and the salesperson must be able to influence the outcomes.

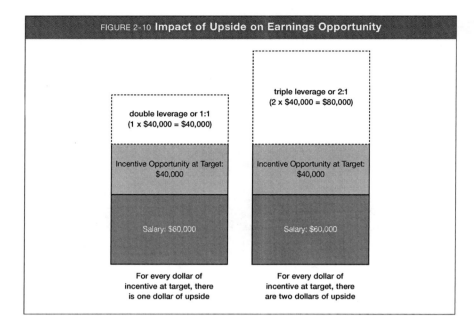

FIGURE 2-10 **Impact of Upside on Earnings Opportunity**

triple leverage or 2:1
(2 x $40,000 = $80,000)

double leverage or 1:1
(1 x $40,000 = $40,000)

Incentive Opportunity at Target:
$40,000

Incentive Opportunity at Target:
$40,000

Salary: $60,000

Salary: $60,000

For every dollar of
incentive at target, there
is one dollar of upside

For every dollar of
incentive at target, there
are two dollars of upside

- Business drivers: Measures should be consistent with the financial drivers associated with successful achievement of the business plan.

- Focus: To ensure focus and meaningful payout opportunity for each measure, it is best to use no more than three performance measures in a sales compensation plan.

- System capabilities: If it cannot be tracked and measured today, it does not belong in the sales compensation plan. Inaccurate or late payouts and reports greatly diminish the motivational power of sales incentive compensation.

Performance measures selected for use in calculating payouts fall into two broad categories:

1. Financial: Since sales jobs are focused on top-line growth and, in some cases, on profitable growth, one measure of success in these jobs must be financial. Financial measures are generally one of two types: volume-based and profitability-based. Sales jobs may be measured against expected productivity or quota. Your rule of thumb should be that between 60 percent and 100 percent of the sales compensation opportunity is based on a sales volume or productivity component. Using this rule ensures that the focus on the sellers is on meeting the company's fiscal plan.

Examples of financial performance measures include the following:

- Sales revenue: overall, by segment or channel, for specific products
- Growth: overall, by customer, account, channel, segment

- Absolute volume, that is, number of units or transactions
- Gross profit: percent, dollars.

Any dollars taken away from financial success reduce the impact of the sales compensation plan on achievement of quantifiable results and thus must be justified as secondary or strategic measures that are critical to the "quality" or nature of financial achievement.

2. Nonfinancial: Nonfinancial measures may be either quantitative or qualitative. Quantitative measures such as market share or share of account are relative rather than absolute and are used in situations where growth is achieved by "taking business" from competitors. Activity measures such as number of calls are quantitative in theory, but qualitative in practice, since only effective activities lead to achievement of financial objectives.

Management by objectives (MBO), also known as key sales objectives or key performance objectives, are examples of nonfinancial, potentially qualitative, objectives. This type of a component is usually point-based and relies on a manager to develop or select from a menu of possible objectives for the seller to achieve over a defined period of time (typically a quarter or half-year). As a rule, these objectives create an averaging of pay for all participants and thus fail to differentiate superior performance. The larger the population for which they are utilized, the less effective and more administratively burdensome they become. They can then be short-lived inside a well-designed sales compensation plan for a large salesforce.

While there are several drawbacks to MBO-like measures, they can be more effective with smaller teams in which the manager is well-trained in objective-setting and evaluation. Further, they force a conversation between the seller and the sales manager about what strategic activities need to occur. They are best used to reward for activities or results that have a high probability of creating a booking or billing in a future period but for which the seller will get no sales credit in the current period (e.g., design wins in an OEM sales model).

Number of Measures

As stated earlier in this section, a rule of thumb is that no sales compensation plan should have more than three components. Using more than three detracts from the value of each measure and the true driving impact of the plan on total sales results. As an adviser to your company, you must always reflect on whether the dollars are significant enough to support more than three measures (especially when those dollars are divided by pay frequency and taxes are subtracted). Too many measurements in a plan often indicate either that a company is trying to design one plan for multiple-distinctive roles or that management lacks agreement on the objectives of the particular sales job.

You will learn more about selecting and prioritizing performance measures in Chapter 4, as part of the design process.

Performance Standards

Another consideration for performance measures used in the sales compensation plan is *performance standards*. As you will see in Chapters 4 and 5, one important task in designing plans is confirming expected performance and establishing two other reference points: one below "expected performance," and one significantly above "expected performance." These three achievement levels are as follows:

- **Threshold:** Threshold is the minimum level of performance that must be achieved before an incentive can be paid.
- **Target:** Target is the expected level of sales results or individual performance. (This is the point at which the target incentive opportunity is earned.)
- **Excellence:** Excellence is the individual sales performance that is in the 90th percentile (top 10 percent) of all performance measured. (This is the point at which the defined "leverage," or upside, is earned.)

Once these three levels are established in a quota-based plan (either bonus or commission), it is then possible to complete the plan payout formula, as well as various analyses such as aggregate plan cost and expected return on investment. Remember: Many people new to sales compensation assume that a defined "excellence" point means that a plan is capped. This is not the case! It simply means that the value of each percent achievement above 100 percent can have a defined value; it does not mean that there is an achievement level above which people cannot earn more sales compensation dollars. When you are working with a design team, or with sales management, it sometimes helps the discussion to refer to the "excellence" point as a "design reference point" that is used for the purpose of developing a payout line and value.

Sales Crediting

One requirement for successful use of any volume measure in the sales compensation plan is well-articulated and well-understood crediting rules. To establish these rules, the sales management team must first have a relatively clear understanding of what customer segments and which products are required to meet the financial plan. Using crediting rules ensures that results that are affected by the salesperson and that support the achievement of your company's business objectives are being tracked and measured. Second, management must take a look at the nature of sales transactions by seller type and consciously determine if all aspects of the transaction provide sales credit toward the volume achievement objective as well as whether they should all be treated equally. In today's complex selling world, all transactions are not alike, and may or may not include all products or services. Further, some are one-time deals instead of ongoing business, which can be paid all at once or over time. Companies thus must know what they need to accomplish and must examine the range of deals that exist in order to determine how to implement crediting toward sales achievement in the core volume component of their plans. Figure 2-11 provides definitions and typical applications of the three kinds of sales credit.

FIGURE 2-11 Sales Crediting		
Type	Definition	Application
Single	One sales resource receives full credit: 100% credit to one person.	One salesperson completes the entire sales process.
Multiple	Full credit provided to two or more sales resources; more than 100% is credited.	A team is required to complete the sale; it is not possible to distinguish the unique contribution of a single resource; the financial impact can be predicted and managed.
Split	The credit is divided in some way among two or more sales resources; 100% credit in total is provided.	Multiple resources or channels may be required to close a sale, but it is relatively easy to distinguish each resource's contribution; additional financial liability is not acceptable.
Partial	A portion of the full credit is allocated to one or more sales resources; less than 100% credit is given in total.	Resources involved in the sale did not contribute as required and full credit is an unacceptable financial liability.

Timing Considerations

Two timing considerations need to be confirmed for the sales compensation plan. The first is the *plan performance period*, the period of time for which the company assigns objectives and measures performance for the purpose of earnings. A plan performance period might be annual (with annual objectives), semi-annual, quarterly, monthly or weekly. In general, the more complex the selling activities and sales cycle, the longer the plan period.

There are two alternative approaches to measurement: cumulative and discrete. A performance measurement is cumulative when the performance of the incumbent is measured over subsequent performance periods. As an example: "While payouts are made each month, performance is cumulative because it is measured from the start of quarter to date." Performance measurement is discrete when the performance of the incumbent is limited to a defined performance period without any connection to past or future performance periods. As an example: "Each month is discrete, because performance is measured for that month and payout is made for that month independent of past or future performance."

The second timing consideration is *payout frequency*, or how often a payout is made. Alternatives range from weekly (generally for those jobs that are paid 100-percent commission) to less frequent payouts (quarterly, for example). The decision to pay more or less frequently should be made after a review of factors such as length of sales cycle, motivational value and the ability of systems to handle payout calculations. You will learn more about timing considerations in Chapter 4.

Alternative Mechanics

The math or formulas used to calculate the payout under the sales compensation plan can be as simple or as complex as the designers wish. Of course, "simpler is better" is a cardinal rule. However, there are many alternatives to consider as the formula is developed. These include both the type of plan that is suitable for the job and the formula modifiers that can be used to ensure that the plan is motivational and financially viable.

Plan Types

The formula by which payout is delivered can be based on two types of plan: commission or bonus. One or both types of plan may be used in the incentive formula, based on the message that management wants to deliver about performance requirements, competitive practice and key business objectives. A commission generally focuses on volume, while a bonus focuses on achievement of one or more specific goals.

Commission is compensation paid as a percentage of sales, measured in either dollars or units. A quota can be used with a commission structure but is not required. The following approaches can be used when designing a commission plan:

- **Single or flat-rate commission:** This is the simplest commission to develop and explain. A fixed rate is applied to all relevant sales in order to calculate the commission payout. For example, 4 percent of sales or $100 per unit. This type of commission is most often used in new companies, companies with very small sales organizations, companies with "open" territories (territories that have no geographic boundaries) or for a new product for which there is no sales history. The theme is, "The more you sell, the more you make."

- **Individual commission rate (ICR):** This approach results in a unique commission rate for each seller. It has two key characteristics in common with a bonus type plan: It has the effect of "evening out" territories in terms of pay, and it is always used with a quota. The theme is, "Every salesperson has the same opportunity to earn their target incentive, no matter how large or small the territory."

- **Tiered (or "ramped") commission structure:** A single rate is determined for "target" achievement, and different rates are provided for sales below target or above target. "Target" may be a specified sales volume, or a percent of quota achievement. If a tiered commission rate is used, the plan can be cumulative or each range can be discrete. If the plan is cumulative, incentive paid vs. incentive earned is recalculated at defined intervals. If the plan is discrete, then the new rate is applied only to dollars associated with the new range of achievement. The theme is, "Sales below target are less valuable than sales at and above target."

- **Adjusted (or "variable") commission rate:** This approach to commission is used if several types of products or types of transactions will be prioritized in the commission structure. The rate applied to each transaction is adjusted based on the priority or importance of the product or transaction. The theme is, "Some sales are more important than others."

Illustrations of each type of commission plan are provided in Figure 2-12.

FIGURE 2-12 **Types of Commissions**		
Type	**Examples**	
Flat Commission: Rate x Volume	• 3% x ($s) • $100/Unit	
Individual Commission Rate (ICR): Individual's Incentive Target divided by Individual's Quota	Rep 1: $100,000 incentive target / $1,000,000 quota = 10% rate applied to sales volume	
	Rep 2: $100,000 incentive target / $1,500,000 quota = 6.7% rate applied to sales volume	
Ramped: Rate Adjusted Based On Achievement Of Sales Volume or Quota	0% – 100% of quota achieved	5% rate
	>100% of quota achieved	7.5% rate
Adjusted: Rate Varies Based on Characteristic Other than Volume or Quota	Product A	5% Base Rate
	Products B and C	7.5% Rate (Base Rate x 1.5)

A bonus is a percent of base pay, or a fixed dollar amount, for accomplishing objectives. A quota or some other kind of goal is generally associated with this type of plan. The three basic approaches to a bonus are as follows:

- **Single- or fixed-rate bonus plan:** One incentive opportunity is available for achieving the specified objective.
- **Interpolated bonus plan:** A formula to calculate a defined dollar value for each percent achievement is used.
- **Step-rate bonus:** A tiered bonus structure, with no interpolation between tiers, is used; each tier is discrete.

Examples of each type of bonus plan are provided in Figure 2-13.

FIGURE 2-13 **Types of Bonus Plans**		
Type	**Examples**	
Fixed	$25,000 for 100% achievement of quota	
Interpolated	0% – 100% of quota achieved	$250 per percent achieved
	>100% of quota achieved	$275 per percent achieved
Step	50% – 99% of quota achieved	$5,000 (no matter where achievement falls in the range)
	99.1% – 102% of quota achieved	$20,000

Modifiers

In addition to selecting the type of plan or plans that will be used in the incentive formula, there are other tools that can be used to adjust how payout is calculated. These include how measures relate to each other for the purposes of payout and how payout is modified (up or down).

Linkage is the factor that relates one measure to another. Measures are linked if payout for one measure depends on attaining another objective. *Unlinked* plans (i.e., plans in which payout for each measure is discrete and has no relationship to achievement in other areas) may indicate to salespeople that they should base their selling priorities on their earnings expectations. Plan designers should consider linking performance measures in the incentive formula if it is desirable for the salesforce to focus on more than one key area and if they use metrics that compete (like market share vs. profitability, etc.). Three mechanisms, as shown in Figure 2-14 on page 43, can do this:

1. A *hurdle* (also known as a *gate*) requires some defined level of achievement in one performance measure before payout is made for another measure.

2. A *multiplier* adjusts payout on one performance measure based on some level of achievement of another measure. Positive adjustment is generally preferred, although adjustment up or down can be used to ensure financial viability of the plan.

3. A *matrix* is the most stringent mechanism, because performance in two areas is used; achievement of one measure is mathematically related to achievement of another to determine payout.

FIGURE 2-14 Linkages

Hurdle

Sales vs. Quota Bonus	
120% of Quota	$40,000
100% of Quota	$30,000
80% of Quota	0

Hurdle: 100% of strategic product quota must be achieved before total sales bonus over target will be paid.

Multiplier

Sales vs. Quota Bonus			Strategic Product Multiplier	
120% of Quota	$40,000	X	>100% of Quota	2.0
100% of Quota	$30,000		100% of Quota	1.5
80% of Quota	0		<100% of Quota	1.0

Matrix

Total Sales			
120%	$20,000	$35,000	$40,000
100%	$10,000	$30,000	$35,000
80%	0	$10,000	$20,000
	80%	100%	120%
		Strategic Product Sales	

Modifiers include both *payout accelerators* and *payout limiters*. While a plan formula could deliver payout on a linear scale, or, with a single rate, most plan designers use both payout limitation and payout acceleration tools to modify the incentive formula.

Payout limitation tools are used to manage cost relative to productivity and are frequently used when a company is new to using sales compensation, setting business goals or allocating quota. The two approaches to payout limitation are a *decelerating payout rate* (the rate for achievement above some defined level decreases) or a *cap* (there is a defined maximum payout available). If a cap is used, it can be applied either to each transaction or to the total payout.

Payout acceleration tools are used to enhance payout above a linear rate for defined levels of overachievement. Acceleration is generally accomplished using specific multipliers against the target incentive opportunity, including adjusted commission rates. In practice, acceleration is the mathematical application of leverage or upside.

Some modifiers may act as either a *decelerator* or *accelerator* depending on achievement levels. For example, a multiplier may adjust payout up or down, based on achievement of the related performance measure. In some cases, additional acceleration is available only if quota is achieved on another measure; payout otherwise remains flat, or has less attractive acceleration. One typical example of this approach is a plan with a financial measure related to quota achievement and another milestone objective such as Design Wins. The qualitative measure would have little or no upside associated with it; however, if it is achieved, the acceleration on overquota payout is greater.

Summing Up

Understanding how sales compensation fits into the total rewards philosophy of your company is a very effective starting point in your involvement in design or redesign efforts. As reinforced in Chapter 4, the key concepts begin with a well-documented and clearly communicated philosophy and guiding principles. The amount of pay available, performance measures, plan formulas and timing of payout are all elements that you will hear about and use in each design process. Figure 2-15 on page 45 gives you a series of questions that provide a framework for structuring your understanding of how the sales compensation plans at your company now work.

- Is everyone on the same sales compensation plan regardless of sales job?

- Do people in similar sales jobs have the same amount of target pay or different amounts? If different, which parts differ – salary, target incentive or target total compensation?

- Of the target compensation, how much is delivered through base salary versus target incentive?

- How many different components or performance measures are used in the sales compensation plan? What are they? What is the relative importance of each component in each plan?

- What percentage of the sales compensation plan is based on sales volume? Is the sales volume component based on quota achievement or absolute dollars?

- For other components, is payout based on quota achievement?

- Is there a minimum or maximum achievement level at which pay begins or is capped? For which component or components?

- What type of plan (commission or bonus) is used to calculate payout for each component?

- Are any of the plan components or measures linked? If so, how?

- How frequently is each component of the sales compensation plan paid?

chapter 3
UNDERSTANDING COMMON PROBLEMS IN SALES COMPENSATION

An effective sales compensation plan can make the difference between top performance and lackluster performance. Companies that operate with high-performing salesforces often report that the sales compensation plan is a major factor in business success. This is the case because these companies have developed the wherewithal to effectively direct, motivate and reward members of the salesforce by means of their sales compensation plans on a consistent, continuous basis. Through good and bad economic times, top-performing companies recognize that aligning the plan with their strategies will increase the likelihood of achieving desired business results. However, successfully maintaining an effective plan poses many challenges.

This chapter identifies seven common problems associated with sales compensation plans and describes how to talk effectively with sales leaders about taking action to resolve these problems if they occur at your company. The list of problems is representative and reflects the most critical challenges perceived by sales leaders, HR/compensation, finance and other corporate functions involved with sales compensation plan design.

The problems are described in the order of their prevalence. For each issue, perspective is provided on why it is common, when or how you are likely to encounter it in working with your sales organizations and alternative approaches you can consider when talking with sales leaders about corrective action. The specific action required to resolve one or more of these problems in your company depends, of course, on the business results that your company has in mind when it revises or completely redesigns its sales compensation plan. There is no one-size-fits-all answer to the question of how one addresses these issues.

This chapter presents the problems in the following sections:

- Missed Financial Objectives
- Sales Employee Dissatisfaction

- Sales Management Frustration
- Exceptions
- Overuse of Sales Contests or SPIFFs
- Plan Framework Does Not Keep Pace With Strategy
- Inadequate Systems Support.

Missed Financial Objectives

A sales compensation plan's principal objective is to direct a company's salespeople to effectively sell to and interact with customers. The expected outcome of doing so is increased volume, a better mix of customers or product sales, improved margins, account retention, more new accounts or some combination of these five results. When a significant percent of the salesforce falls short of achieving assigned financial targets, that shortfall may be a sign that the sales compensation plan is misaligned with the required financial outcomes. Missed financial targets are most commonly associated with an ineffective plan because top managers look to the plan to communicate growth, profit and strategic requirements to the salesforce. The greater the amount of compensation at risk, through commission, bonus or both, the higher the expectation that salesforce members will alter their behavior to achieve stated financial and other targets. Thus, when financial targets are not met, top managers think first of sales compensation as the likely culprit.

There are, however, other factors that can contribute to missed financial targets. These factors include the following:

- Overly ambitious sales-growth targets (e.g., quotas substantially greater than those for the prior year, market growth or both) that are not built on a clear understanding of sales potential and capacity
- Overassignment of the company's targets (i.e., assigning additional points to each succeeding level of allocation, resulting in an aggregate that is significantly higher than the company's goal)
- Poor quota allocation that does not consider where growth is likely to occur (customers and products)
- Product or service shortcomings such as lack of on-time delivery, incomplete order fulfillment and out-of-stock/back-order situations
- Competitive price-cutting, whether through planned promotions or discretionary discounts.

It is not unusual to encounter the problem of the sales compensation plan being blamed for missed financial targets in a sales culture in which the plan functions as the "phantom manager." Of course, no plan can replace effective sales leadership. Therefore, when the sales compensation plan is being blamed for missed financial targets, it is important to understand how much of this problem is actually the plan's fault. One way to gain that understanding is to engage sales leaders in a discussion about the circumstances surrounding the missed financial target. Figure 3-1 is a list of discussion questions that you can use to initiate that conversation with sales leaders in your company.

FIGURE 3-1 **Discussion Questions**

- What are the factors that you believe are causing the salesforce to miss its financial targets?

- Which of these factors are directly associated with the sales compensation plan?

- What changes in the compensation plan, if made, do you feel will direct, motivate and reward for course-correcting sales results?

- What primary complaints do you hear from your sales team regarding the sales compensation plan and its administration?

- What aspects of the sales compensation plan are working well?

- If you could have done any one thing differently with this year's sales compensation plan, what would that have been?

With information gleaned from discussing these questions, you can help sales leaders appropriately determine how much of the problem of missed financial targets is due to the sales compensation plan, and assist them in identifying specific plan elements that should be reviewed and possibly changed.

Sales Employee Dissatisfaction

As a general rule, sales employees judge a sales compensation plan by a single criterion: Can they make as much or more money under the new plan as they did under the former plan if they change their behavior consistent with the stated business strategy? However, salespeople recognize that the competitive marketplace is dynamic and that their companies must respond to the changing environment in order to sustain profitable growth. Thus, the majority of salespeople expect that their sales compensation plans will undergo at least some change on an annual basis. Assuming that the incentive compensation opportunity is not decreased, plan change by itself is not a principal source of sales employee dissatisfaction.

The principal sources of dissatisfaction with the compensation plan are actually related to what is changed and how a company goes about making those changes. The most common sources are as follows:

- Quota assignment, particularly when there is no explanation about how it was determined
- Threshold performance, particularly when it is set so high (e.g., 90+ percent) that a significant number of salespeople realize at the outset of the year that they will not be "in the money"
- Overly complex incentive formulas that make performing self-calculation difficult or impossible
- Inaccurate sales crediting that results in shadow accounting by sellers, continual recalculation of results and inordinately late payment of expected incentive earnings
- Significant delay (e.g., 90 days to 120 days after the year begins) in communicating the new plan's details so that members of the salesforce can estimate or project their annual incentive earnings based on their own performance scenarios
- Frequent changes to the plan during the business year without a clear explanation of their meaning.

One way to determine if your company has a salesforce dissatisfaction problem because of its sales compensation plan is to routinely survey the salesforce about change. It is a wise practice to ask salespeople how they feel about a plan shortly after they have received their first payment under that new plan. Figure 3-2 on page 53 provides an illustrative survey to obtain information about perceptions. It can be used throughout the design process.

No doubt there are other questions that could be asked of the salesforce through such a survey. However, these questions represent a good starting point. Salesforce dissatisfaction with compensation plan change is quite frequently based on hearsay or anecdotes. With survey information in hand, you can help sales leaders determine the extent to which dissatisfaction is a problem and the best prospects for addressing the causes. This approach enables both HR management and sales management to verify that these areas of dissatisfaction are not merely attempts to negotiate unjustifiably better terms or higher payouts.

Sales Management Frustration

A sales compensation plan should complement a company's sales management process. A common source of frustration among field sales managers is a lack of alignment between what the sales compensation plan pays for and what they believe salesforce members must do to achieve sales success as defined by the business strategy. A lack of alignment between the performance measures used

FIGURE 3-2 **Salesforce Survey Questions**

INFORMATION ABOUT YOU

1. Your position: ☐ Region Manager   ☐ Account Manager   ☐ Inside Sales Specialist
2. Your region: ☐ North Central   ☐ Midwest   ☐ South Central   ☐ West

YOUR OVERALL COMMENTS ABOUT THE NEW SALES COMPENSATION PLAN

Questions	Check One Response		
	Yes	No	Unsure
1. My immediate supervisor thoroughly explained to me how I could earn commission under the new plan.			
2. I understand my new compensation plan.			
3. I understand the plan terms and conditions.			
4. Generally speaking, I believe that the new sales compensation plan is better than the prior year's plan.			
5. I see alignment between our business strategy and how I am paid.			
6. My sales goal (quota) for the year is realistic.			
7. Generally speaking, achieving my sales goal for the year is important to me.			
8. I have a good understanding of how my commission is calculated under the new compensation plan.			
9. I believe that my pay is calculated correctly.			
10. Top-performing members of the salesforce here earn significantly more compensation.			
11. Since the new compensation plan was introduced, I have changed my selling behavior so I can optimize my payout opportunity.			
12. I expect to earn more compensation under the new plan than I did under last year's plan.			

LIKES/DISLIKES ABOUT SPECIFIC PLAN FEATURES

1. What do you like MOST about the new compensation plan? (Check only three choices)

☐ Simplicity	☐ Size of incentive opportunity at target and upside
☐ (Fewer) performance measures	☐ Goals (quotas) more realistic
☐ Threshold (lower than prior year)	☐ No cap
☐ Other (write in)	

2. What do you like LEAST about the new compensation plan? (Check only three choices)

☐ Simplicity	☐ Size of incentive opportunity at target and upside
☐ (Fewer) performance measures	☐ Goals (quotas) more realistic
☐ Threshold (lower than prior year)	☐ No cap
☐ Other (write in)	

Do you have other comments or observations about the new sales compensation plan that you would like to share with the leadership team?

in salesforce and sales management plans is another source of frustration. For example, if the current sales compensation plan rewards for volume growth (i.e., if all sales dollars are equal regardless of customers or products sold), members of the salesforce will be indifferent to where and how they achieve sales. However, when sales success for the year requires profitable, balanced product-line selling, their selling efforts and the efforts of their immediate sales managers must be aligned. The compensation plan must support that strategy for both the sellers and their managers. As sales managers well know, members of the salesforce devote their time and energy to the things that determine their pay. Some salespeople will disregard the direction they are given if it is not reinforced through the compensation plan.

You are likely to encounter this problem when a representative sample of field sales managers is not involved in the sales compensation plan design process. In addition to involving field sales managers in the design process, and before launching a new or changed plan, it is a good idea to survey field managers relative to any proposed change that is significant. Figure 3-3 presents questions that field sales managers could be asked about a new or revised plan before it is launched.

FIGURE 3-3 Field Manager Perceptions of Sales Compensation Plans and Administration Effectiveness (Rate 1-5, Disagree to Agree)

- I believe that I can explain the new plan correctly and show my people how to "win" under it.

- I believe that the proposed plan is consistent with the sales direction to my people.

- The plan supports all of the behaviors we need for effective selling and customer-relationship management.

- I believe that the plan will be effective in motivating and rewarding my people.

- The plan allows me to attract and retain the talent I need to compete in this market.

- Our plan communication materials are effective for new hires as well as existing employees.

Responses to these questions provide information about field sales managers' support for the changed or new plan. The resulting insight is particularly important because research shows that how field sales managers feel about the sales compensation plan materially impacts the salesforce's attitudes toward the plan. To minimize or eliminate the problem of sales manager frustration with the plan, the design team should seek the involvement of field sales managers in the design process. Their support for the new or changed plan should be confirmed prior to plan launch.

Exceptions

There is no perfect sales compensation plan. The business situation in which a company finds itself largely contributes to a plan's effectiveness. It is not unusual for an organization to make exceptions to plan rules from time to time when the business situation changes. For example, when a major economic downturn occurs and business forecasts are adjusted downward, a company might make an exception to the plan with an adjustment of quotas. If the business unit is given "plan relief," the salesforce in turn is given "quota relief." This type of exception is not regarded as a problem.

Problem exceptions are those that involve the failure to apply consistent rules to the calculation of sales incentive compensation (either commission or bonus). The result of such an exception is generally payment that is out of alignment with performance. The functional department charged with the responsibility of calculating sales incentive payments typically keeps track of exceptions made in the payment process. The number, frequency and types of exceptions made to plan rules compared to that of prior years should be examined regularly. For example, an increase in the percentage of the salesforce that has been affected by exceptions over a period of a few years is a clear signal that the sales compensation plan, or a related process such as sales crediting, may be failing.

You are likely to observe the problem of numerous exceptions when the plan includes measures that are not aligned with the sales cycle, measures that are not supported by systems, very high quotas or calculations and crediting rules that are either not supported or not understood by sales management and the salesforce.

Overuse of Sales Contests or SPIFFs

Sales contests are short-term incentive programs designed to motivate members of the salesforce to accomplish specific sales objectives. Some companies refer to these programs as SPIFFs (special performance incentive for the field force). Essentially, sales contests are a supplement to a company's compensation plan. As such, they should be a complement to the salesforce's primary performance objectives, not a distraction. Common sales contest objectives include the following:

- Stimulate specific, existing product sales.
- Introduce new products.
- Acquire new customers.
- Emphasize higher-profit products.
- Overcome a seasonal slump.

- Take advantage of a competitor's temporary market weakness.
- Stimulate overall volume early in a quarter or year.

Like any motivational sales tool, sales contests are effective when used correctly. Effectiveness is measured by determining whether sales results – as a direct result of the contest – exceed previous projections. However, there are situations where contests are overused and, in effect, compete with or overtake the economic value of the sales incentive compensation plan. When the number of contests conducted during a year increases substantially over the prior year, or when the percent of incentive earnings from contest winning becomes a significant percent of sales incentive compensation (e.g., greater than 10 percent of W2 earnings), the compensation plan itself may be failing.

Plan Framework Does Not Keep Pace with Strategy

A *plan framework* is the structure of a sales compensation plan prior to the final determination of payout rates, sales credit definitions and so forth. Generally speaking, four elements define a sales compensation plan's framework: total cash compensation, salary/incentive ratio or mix (and thus the amount of the incentive opportunity), leverage (the upside compensation opportunity associated with performance overachievement) and the performance measures and standards. When a company alters its sales strategy (customers it markets to, the products it offers, the sales channels and jobs deployed), there are likely to be implications for one or more elements of the compensation framework. In such a circumstance, not changing the framework of the plan can be a problem that contributes to its failure.

Inadequate Systems Support

For the salesforce, the sales compensation plan is all about cash flow. This means that being paid accurately and on time for what is sold is of vital importance to salespeople. The inability of a company to pay members of the salesforce correctly and on time is frequently due to inadequate IT systems support for payment calculation. Essentially, the problem is that plan designers have not carefully determined what performance measures can or cannot be tracked and credited through automated systems for the purpose of incentive compensation determination. The result is that calculation must then rely on manual processes. These processes result in increased administrative expense as well as errors that are not caught until after members of the salesforce are paid. The result is that salespeople are either underpaid or overpaid.

You are likely to encounter the problem of inadequate systems support for the sales compensation plan in situations where there may have been numerous changes in the sales organization structure. This is typically the result of business acquisitions/mergers, new product acquisition or development, implementation of new sales channels or some combination of all of these changes. The problem of inadequate support often occurs when existing or legacy systems cannot properly credit the salesforce under the new structure. Avoiding or resolving problems of inadequate support requires a strong collaborative effort by several functions, including sales, finance, HR/compensation and IT. Software companies specializing in administration of sales compensation plans have recently appeared in the market, but some companies have encountered new problems associated with their use. Choose carefully (interview references, etc.) when selecting an outside vendor to help your company solve its systems support problems.

Helping Sales Leaders Overcome Common Problems

When one or more of these seven common problems are in play within a salesforce, the sales compensation plan's effectiveness may be substantially at risk. It is thus important for sales leaders to act quickly and decisively to resolve problems before it is too late. Unfortunately, sales management is often too slow to act because it fears the consequences of a change in the sales compensation plan. The most common concerns of sales leaders are that: 1) the company will lose top-producing sales representatives, 2) the salesforce will become confused over the business' direction and 3) salespeople will lose motivation and productivity during the transition period (the period during which they try to figure out what the new plan directs them to do and how it rewards them). These are legitimate concerns that provide an opportunity for the HR/compensation professional to work with sales leaders to help them define the problem (actual vs. perceived in many cases) and develop a plan of action.

Summing Up

There are many potential problems associated with sales compensation, ranging from missed business targets to inadequate systems. As we described in this chapter, many typical problems are actually caused by multiple factors and are not simply the result of having "the wrong plan" or misapplying the plan. However, in order to address and resolve perceived problems with the plan, you must understand where the problems have occurred, to what degree they are problems with plan design or implementation and what other functions should be involved in their resolution.

chapter 4
PARTICIPATING IN THE DESIGN PROCESS

IV

Sales compensation is a dynamic and valuable management tool. In Chapter 3, we described common problems associated with sales compensation plans. In your role as the HR professional, you may be asked to work with a team to address such problems or to participate in the design of a new sales compensation plan. Depending on the traditions in your company, other resources that are available, stakeholders in the process and management requirements, your role may vary from team member to subject-matter expert to process leader. However, whatever your role, a key factor to design success is following a thoughtful, well-structured and well-facilitated design process. Doing so ensures that the company's business objectives are appropriately reflected in the compensation plan. Because the design process follows generally accepted principles and best practices in sales compensation design, it provides assurance that deliverables are effective and well-aligned with company needs. The key steps in this process and the role an HR professional should play are described in the following sections:

- Process Importance and Benefits
- Process Participants
- The Design Process.

Process Importance and Benefits

Sales compensation is by its very nature extremely tactical. This is because the plan defines and communicates what members of the salesforce have to do to earn their pay. As such, it is critical to ensuring alignment between the company's key strategic objectives and the sales organization's required behaviors. The success of the program requires agreement on concepts, principles and plan details among those subject to the plan and other critical stakeholders – particularly sales management, finance, human resources and product marketing. Using a well-structured design process provides a platform for gaining agreement across and within these crucial decision makers and users. It also creates a foundation for plan-design work that can be readily referenced and replicated in the future.

The process can also provide motivation and rationale for teaming between functions and staff members that may not have worked together on the sales compensation plan in prior periods. A design process brings together multidisciplinary skills and experiences with a well-defined road map that considers current issues, future needs and the application of generally accepted principles of effective design. Companies that are the most satisfied with their sales compensation plans ensure that shortcuts are not taken in the plan-design process. When shortcuts are used because of insufficient time, inexperienced resources or incomplete knowledge of jobs, the result is often a flawed plan that does not help management achieve desired business results.

Process Participants

The design team may be either an ad hoc team or a permanent, standing sales compensation team that is accountable for the process of plan review, new plan design, plan modeling and costing, and plan communication. Membership on the team is typically not a full-time assignment. The team includes representatives from all functions that could be considered stakeholders (i.e., all functions that are accountable for achievement of the business plan). Team members also include those who are accountable for various aspects of plan design, analysis, communication, administration and documentation.

In some companies, the responsibility for assembling the team and managing the design process is a key HR responsibility. In others, HR is a valued member of the team. If neither is the case in your company, lack of participation could be due to one or more of the factors described in Chapter 1. Regardless of the reason, the lack of HR involvement in the process has significant drawbacks for the organization. Human resources key accountabilities typically include both benefits and compensation programs, so the function generally includes knowledgeable compensation professionals. In addition, HR is the function that is the custodian of consistency with corporate policies and philosophy, legal requirements, and industry regulations and practices. HR therefore represents a critical center of responsibility within the process. Experience in process development and facilitation is crucial to the success of the design team, and these are skills that the HR professional can provide. Finally, the sales organization is the company's point of contact with its customers and, as such, HR should serve to ensure that the compensation plan contributes to both an appropriate sales culture and compliance with business ethics.

Whether HR or compensation's role is that of process leader or team member, it is important that core functional areas are represented on the team, either throughout the process or as ad hoc members for key tasks and deliverables.

The design and process teams should be cross-functional and should include representatives from the following departments (in addition to HR):

- **Sales management** (first- or second-line). Team members should ensure that the plan is appropriate for the jobs covered by it, that it motivates and rewards the correct behaviors, that it is a useful management tool and that it supports achievement of business objectives.

- **Finance.** Team members should be accountable for assessing the financial viability of the plan and its consistency with corporate objectives. Finance may also assist with plan analytics such as assessment (on the front end) and costing (to finalize the design).

- **Sales administration.** Team members may complete plan assessments and ensure that sales crediting, tracking, reporting and results-analysis systems are in place.

- **Marketing.** Team members may participate as ad hoc members based on requirements for specific product or customer-segment plan components.

- **IT.** Team members working with sales administration should ensure that tracking, measurement and reporting systems are tested and verified prior to plan rollout and that they provide adequate support for the new plan. These members may also be actively involved in evaluating internally developed or externally provided tools or services used to ensure this capability.

Because of the strategic and tactical importance of the design process and outcomes, a frequent question is, "Shouldn't key executives participate as members in the design team?" The answer is that executives at the "C" level (chief sales officer, chief financial officer, chief HR officer) are more typically members of a steering committee that reviews the recommendations of the design team. When the team plans significant plan changes, you should consider the option of forming a steering committee that has the responsibility of organizing the team and determining objectives for it to address, providing strategic direction at key points in the process and making decisions about key issues or questions. The entire design team and the steering committee should also be chartered to represent both their own positions and the specific strategies and objectives of the sales organization.

The Design Process

After management has chartered a design team and selected its members, the team can turn its attention to the actual design process. An important first step is explaining the design process' structure and importance, the company's total rewards philosophy, the design team's chartered objectives, the time frame for the process and the key deliverables. HR should take responsibility for this presentation.

The entire design process may take weeks or months; the length of time needed depends on the extent and significance of the changes. However, the process described here is applicable when the current plan needs to be only tweaked (i.e., relatively minor changes need to be made); when a plan is being developed for the first time; and when significant change is required because of new jobs, new strategies, market changes or corporate changes such as mergers or acquisitions.

Step 1: Clarify Business Objectives and Strategic Initiatives

The primary goal of any sales compensation plan is to support the achievement of key business objectives and the strategic initiatives of the organization for the plan year. Therefore, the critical first step is clarification of crucial financial, product, market and strategic goals. The steering committee is the resource that will provide leadership and guidance to the design team in this area. The team should have a good understanding of the current plan and the primary objectives the plan was designed to support. Questions that the design team should ask the steering committee must be as specific and to-the-point as the following questions:

- What is our growth plan for next year? In what markets or with what products?
- What are the expectations of the sales organization, and of each job in the organization, for achieving those goals?
- Do we have strategic, nonfinancial objectives that will be given to the salesforce?

Step 2: Assess Current Plans

When the design initiative is not focused on developing a plan for the first time, the design team should allocate time to qualitatively and quantitatively assessing the current plan. You will learn more about this step in Chapter 5, which provides you with concepts, tools and techniques associated with plan assessment. As a process leader or participant, you may be asked (or you may ask others) to play key roles in that assessment. As the HR professional on the team, it will be your responsibility to (1) review and assess target pay levels, (2) review and assess the terms and conditions of the plan and (3) ensure consistency with legal regulations, corporate policies and other related practices. It will also be your responsibility to provide advice to the team, based on your previous experience in plan design, on recommended design approaches.

Step 3: Define Objectives of the Sales Compensation Plan

In some organizations, it is important to carefully consider both what the sales compensation plan should do and what it should not do. Compensation plans are a key management tool, but they do not take the place of management assessment, personnel development and training. Thoughtful consideration must be given to developing and documenting the most significant objectives that the plan will be designed to meet. These objectives are supplemental to the generic (but important) "attract, retain and motivate members of the salesforce" and "be consistent with competitive practice," but are just as important. Specific financial goals such as "support profitable growth" or "motivate achievement of new product introduction goals," and qualitative goals such as "reward entry into key market segments," should be clearly defined and documented. See Figure 4-1 for an example of a statement of plan objectives. Additional information about defining plan objectives is provided in Chapter 6.

FIGURE 4-1 **One Company's Statement of Commission Plan Objectives**

The purpose of this program is to attract, retain, motivate and reward key contributors relative to accomplishment of goals and objectives in support of the overall business plan and strategy. The commission plan is designed to establish a direct link between the achievement of our aggressive sales targets (for key products A and B) and individual rewards. The plan will recognize and reward individuals that successfully collaborate with team members to achieve their sales plan within specific markets. By design, the commission plan will provide opportunities for market-competitive rewards for achievement of sales and margin-performance targets, and above-market rewards for outstanding performance that exceeds the target objectives.

Step 4: Assess Eligibility of Jobs

As described in Chapter 2, the design process should always include an assessment (or reassessment) of eligibility to participate in the sales compensation plan. While sales management may view this step as a straightforward task, the following factors must be considered when determining eligibility:

• Changes in the sales process

• Addition or subtraction of jobs

• Change in job accountabilities.

Step 5: Establish Compensation Levels

As an HR professional, you are in an ideal position to provide direct and valuable input into this very critical step in the design process. Because sales compensation terms can vary from company to company, you should ensure that the design team is "speaking the same language" when you provide recommendations in this area. Key terms were defined and discussed in Chapter 2. However, it is important to use the terminology that is acceptable in your company and your industry (e.g., your company may refer to target earnings as OTE rather than TCC).

This step requires an objective and balanced approach to determining both the target earnings (target cash compensation) for each job and the amount of that pay that is at risk. In addition, the amount of extra earnings that are available for overtarget performance must be determined. You should ensure that all factors are considered in establishing or confirming compensation. To do so, you should develop your recommendations sequentially: TCC, mix, upside. Chapter 5 provides significant details about tools and resources for completing this task.

Step 6: Select Performance Measures and Determine Weighting

Once you have helped the team determine how much to pay, you need to help it determine for what pay will be made. Selection of key performance measures is always a balancing act, but one rule of thumb is "no more than three is optimal, five is the maximum." A second rule of thumb is that the plan must use measures that can be accurately tracked and measured, or that result in outcomes that are consistently and objectively observable and can be documented. Use of multiple, disparate, low-value measures significantly dilutes the motivational and directional aspects of the plan, and should therefore be avoided. A typical plea is, "Let's add it to the incentive plan to be sure the members of the salesforce focus on it." Questions that need to be answered in this case are as follows:

1. Does it belong in the incentive plan or in a total sales-performance management assessment?

2. Can we track, measure and report results accurately at the required frequency?

As described in Chapter 2, several types of measures can be considered for the sales compensation plan. However, the single most important measure should be financial – volume or profit in dollars or as a percent of quota. Secondary measures can include productivity or strategic metrics that focus the salesforce on qualitative or longer-term objectives. A simple way to think about the categories of measures is as follows:

1. **Volume first** (at the most relevant level of measurement – individual, team, company)

2. **Profit to fund** (e.g., gross margin, gross profit, mix of business) only at appropriate levels of the organization

3. **Productivity** (to measure improvement in return on sales investment)

4. **Strategic objectives** (for jobs where quantitative results are hard to measure

due to lack of history or lack of systems, or for jobs that must focus primarily or exclusively on long-term strategic efforts).

Once measures have been selected, they must be prioritized according to importance – the most visible way to do so is by weighting the measures, that is, assigning each a value as a proportion of 100, or 100 percent of the incentive opportunity at target. An illustration of weighting is provided in Figure 4-2. A rule of thumb is that no measure should ever be worth less than 10 percent of the incentive opportunity. The reason for this rule is easily illustrated by performing a calculation of the amount of pay designated by 10 percent of target incentive, dividing it by the payout frequency and then subtracting taxes. The amount typically is not meaningful enough to motivate behavior.

FIGURE 4-2 **Weighted Performance Measures**		
Performance Measure	Weight	Opportunity at Target*
Territory Volume vs. Quota	60	$24,000
Team Volume vs. Quota	20	$ 8,000
Strategic Objectives	20	$ 8,000
	Total: 100	$40,000

Step 7: Develop the Plan Formula

Chapter 2 explained the fundamentals of sales compensation design, including alternative mechanics. It is at this point in the design process that those alternatives will be considered for each plan component. For each relevant job, the team now knows what performance measures will be the basis for payout and how much each is worth. The mechanics are the delivery mechanism used to calculate payout for each component and in total, based on whether measures are linked or unlinked. The plan formula is likely to go through several versions, based on plan modeling. Key plan decisions will need to address the following:

• Incentive plan type for each plan component: bonus or commission, and what type

• Performance range: Target, threshold, excellence

• Formula modifiers: Accelerators, caps, linkages.

The HR representative on the team is typically charged with ensuring that the measures are consistent with corporate philosophy; that they are aligned with the type of behavior that the plan seeks to motivate and reward; and that they meet legal and ethical requirements. The sales leaders are generally responsible for determining that the measures are aligned with the year's business objectives, that they accurately reflect job responsibilities and that they are consistent with the salesforce member's ability to achieve results. Established guiding principles, as discussed in Chapter 2, will assist HR and the sales leaders in these activities.

Step 8: Determine Performance Measurement and Payout Periods

As discussed in Chapter 2, the plan performance period is the time period over which sales results are measured and credited. Payout frequency is the time period for which the company makes a payout. These two periods (performance and payout) may or may not be the same. For example, many sales compensation plans in the business-to-business sales world are annual plans with year-to-date performance and payout calculations. In the retail world, or in other highly transactional selling environments, the performance period could be monthly or even weekly, and payout occurs at the end of the performance period for results delivered during that period alone.

To determine the preferred performance period, various criteria are considered, including the following:

- Type of job, including number of sales transactions, size of sales transactions and length of sales cycle
- Type and maturity of product, including ability to forecast accurately and build reliable quotas
- Desired salesforce behavior.

Once the performance period has been confirmed, the payout period/payout frequency is the next design decision. While several factors impact this decision as well, perhaps the single most important criterion for the salesforce is cash flow. Frequent payout meets this need, as does the motivational principle that payout close to the event is a stronger positive reinforcement than delayed payout. High-paying sales jobs (>$100,000) and low-mix roles (<80/20) typically have less concern about cash flow than lower-paying jobs with high mixes (inside sales, etc.). However, it is critical to establish payout frequency that truly reflects performance, as well. Therefore, many companies with long-term plan-performance periods (e.g., annual year-to-date plans) provide for a monthly or quarterly "progress" payment against year-to-date performance.

Step 9: Complete Cost Analysis and Determine Earnings Impact

The plan cannot be considered final until the design has been financially tested. Therefore, a cost analysis and individual impact analysis must be completed, because design features such as performance ranges and formula details may need to be changed. Key team members for these analyses are representatives from sales administration and finance; HR assistance is likely to be needed to ensure complete and current employee data is available for the analyses.

The first set of analyses to complete is plan costing, which estimates combined overall plan cost using the new plan formula and the projected participant count for each plan for the plan year. This analysis determines whether the payout curve, related results and probable return are consistent with the plan objectives as agreed to by the design team and steering committee. To complete this activity, a financial impact or costing model should be developed. This model estimates payout vs. productivity while keeping most variables (e.g., base pay, target incentive pay) constant. The basis used for the analysis is frequently either history (the performance distribution for the previous year for this group of incumbents) or market practice (the market expectation for distribution of performance in a particular job). Based on your company's needs, more complex models that consider variables in addition to headcount, quota and past performance may also be developed.

Individual plan modeling generally compares payout under the old plan to payout under the new plan on a person-by-person basis using each person's historical performance. This approach is also sometimes used to cost a plan, but it requires that all plan components remain essentially similar to the previous year's plan and that target compensation levels are not significantly changed. Another approach to individual plan modeling, particularly for new jobs, involves alternative scenario modeling, in which a person's achievement of X means payment of Y. Whatever approach is used, this analysis is important for the process of determining the impact of plan change on each employee.

Step 10: Finalize and Launch Plan
The plan is done, that is, the design has been completed, tested, perhaps revised, and it appears to support everything required by the steering committee. At this point, the design team must deal with administrative accountabilities, if they have not previously been addressed. That is, the company function, and what roles in that function, that will be responsible for plan administration, including performance tracking, measuring and reporting, sales crediting, payout calculations and payouts, must be determined.

If your organization does not have a formal approval process for the sales compensation plan, establishing one now should be seriously considered. Having such a process provides for one final opportunity for input and questions about the plan. In the current business climate of increased corporate regulation and oversight (i.e., Sarbanes-Oxley), it is important to make clear who in the company has the responsibility for the approval of the sales compensation plan. Chapter 9 covers plan governance guidelines and principles. However, a key rule of thumb is this: Because a sales compensation plan can have a direct and material impact on a company's financial statements, it is imperative that approval authority is explicitly stated.

For example, your design team could first present the plans and related costing to the steering committee one more time, along with a summary of the expected benefits, and perhaps the potential drawbacks of the plan. Additionally, contemporary practice indicates that a sales compensation plan requires the approval of the chief sales officer, the CFO, legal counsel and the chief HR officer (or that person's corporate compensation delegate).

After the plan has received formal approval from top management, it is typically the responsibility of HR to take the lead in preparing plan documentation. Other departments – finance, legal and sales operations – often are involved in the review and finalization of the documentation effort. The documentation should include the terms and conditions (T&Cs), as well as a clear description of the sales compensation plan components and how they work (including payout examples). The paperwork may be prepared as two separate documents. Particularly in organizations with several jobs eligible for sales compensation, one T&C document can describe the employment, crediting and other policies that influence plan participation and payout.

When the plan is launched, documentation is important, but does not represent the only tools and communication media that will help the plan succeed. Top-down communication is essential and starts with a leadership message (in a memo, Webcast or blanket e-mail) to set the stage for the plan. Additional tools may include a Frequently Asked Questions (FAQs) and the answers for managers to use; a "management cheat sheet" that summarizes the most important changes from the previous plan (or, for new plans, the most important points about the plan); and several examples of how the plan works (e.g., using a "payout estimator" in Excel). Best practices actually provide managers with the data and individual earnings differential results for their direct reports. This helps managers avoid doing that work themselves and prevents salespeople from spending valuable selling time on creating their own comparison.

Summing Up

A well-defined and effectively facilitated sales compensation design process is critical to ensuring that the plan reflects alignment between the goals of the business and the mechanics used to reward the salesforce for achieving results. Whether the role of human resources is as a team member or the process leader, there are several significant tasks for which the HR professional should take the lead. First, the HR professional should encourage the use of a multifunctional approach to the design of the sales compensation plan. This is important not only because of the requirement of Sarbanes-Oxley, but because such an approach provides the opportunity to integrate important marketing, sales and financial goals within the plan.

Next, HR should take the lead on or actively participate in the development and use of a design process. This chapter suggested a practical, action-oriented process that the HR professional or another process owner can tailor and modify according to the needs of a particular company. Finally, HR should help make clear the roles of various functions – for example, sales, marketing, finance – in the design process. While it is important that everyone understands that the sales department is accountable for an effective sales compensation plan, other functions have a responsibility to weigh in on the plan to ensure that it contributes to the achievement of agreed-upon company objectives.

chapter 5

ASSESSING CURRENT PLAN EFFECTIVENESS

V

Chapter 3 explained why and how sales compensation plans become obsolete over time. Because they do become obsolete, companies that have an existing plan in place should perform a complete assessment of it before designing a new one. The common sales compensation plan problems discussed in Chapter 3 may be self-evident when they are uncovered, but in most cases, their root causes are not easily identified and documented. It is common for companies to set out to correct a behavioral or strategic issue by changing the compensation plan when the cause of the problem exists "upstream" from where the salesforce operates. For example, shortcomings in the articulation of strategy, fundamental definition of market segments, approach to product launch or description and staffing of sales roles may have more to do with a failing compensation plan than the plan design itself.

Chapter 4 described a process that uses well-defined roles that may go off track if not based on a clear, complete assessment. A clear process and role-based framework is not just key to speed and efficiency; it is a road map for balancing cross-functional challenges. The assessment of your current sales compensation plan is the time and place to set out on the right foot for any redesign effort. This chapter describes the following elements related to assessing an existing sales compensation plan:

- Preparing for the Assessment
- Data and Analytics
- External Surveys and Benchmarking Analysis
- Qualitative Assessment – Interviews and Surveys
- Administrative Assessment.

Preparing for the Assessment
One of the first decisions to make in preparing for a complete sales compensation assessment regards timing. As the HR professional working with the sales team, you should recommend beginning at least five months prior to the new plan year.

Doing this provides first half-year sales data for performance evaluation and typically more insight into the following year's sales model and objectives than the team would receive in starting earlier. For a company on a calendar year, this implies that the summer is spent examining performance to date and contemplating the next year's business plan, go-to-market model and organizational structure.

It is also critical to secure the necessary time commitment from internal and external resources for the sales compensation plan assessment. The assessment team should have 60 percent to 80 percent overlap (consistent membership) with the team that will go forward later in the design process. It should have representation from finance, sales management and HR (potentially also including IT, legal, marketing and sales operations), and membership should be capped at eight to 10 people. You may find it hard to limit this group, given the topic, and should ask senior management's support in determining the final team. Another strategy might be to have key stakeholder groups select/nominate representatives to serve on the team. Once the assessment team is appointed and everyone understands his or her role, you are ready to pull together a data request.

Data and Analytics

Objective, quantitative performance and pay data are extremely important to the assessment process. The rule of thumb is that one full year of historical incumbent data is a minimum requirement for a sound assessment. Depending on the time of year the assessment commences and the history of plan changes, this may mean the last 12 months of data, the previous full fiscal year, annualized current-year data or more. In businesses with long sales cycles (greater than six months), it is typically more important to have a full fiscal year of data than it would be for transactional businesses due to the uneven nature of contract signings and revenue flow. If a midyear plan change took place in the previous fiscal year, it will be a challenge to piece together representative performance and pay data so that the current plans can be assessed.

Incumbent pay and performance data, quota data and employment data should be collected at the beginning of the sales compensation plan assessment process. Figure 5-1 on page 77 describes the data fields that should be included in the file of each incumbent who held an eligible sales role in the previous year.

Several calculated fields should be added to the data fields. First, previous-year performance percentage should be derived by dividing previous-year actual performance by previous-year goals. A field for previous-year pay percentage should be created by dividing previous-year total actual compensation by previous-year target total compensation. These first two calculated fields

FIGURE 5-1 Incumbent Pay and Performance Data

- Sales Representative Name
- Sales Representative ID#
- Region
- Supervisor
- Job Title/Plan Title
- Date of Hire (important if there is a question about the impact of seniority on performance and pay)
- Termination Date (important if there is a fundamental question about turnover and sales compensation's impact on employee retention)
- Previous-Year Base Salary
- Previous-Year Target Commissions or Bonuses (by measure or program)
- Previous-Year Target Total Compensation (TTC)

- Previous-Year Goals (revenue, profit, units, etc.)
- Previous-Year Actual Attainment (revenue, profit, units, etc.)
- Previous-Year Actual Base Salary Paid
- Previous-Year Actual Commissions or Bonuses Paid (by measure or program)
- Previous-Year Total Actual Cash Compensation (W2)
- Current-Year Base Salary
- Current-Year Target Commissions or Bonuses (by measure or program)
- Current-Year TTC
- Current-Year Goals (revenue, profit, units, etc.)

support your first assessment analytic – pay:performance correlation. (See Figure 5-2.) Performed on a job-by job basis where there is sufficient full-year incumbent population to create a meaningful analysis, this analysis helps the plan-design team understand the integrity of the formula mechanics your company has had in place under previous plans.

FIGURE 5-2 Example of Pay:Performance Correlation

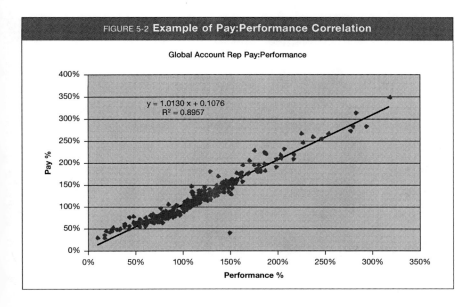

Global Account Rep Pay:Performance

$y = 1.0130\,x + 0.1076$
$R^2 = 0.8957$

Pay:performance correlation is most easily accomplished through a scatter plot in Microsoft Excel with performance % as the X-axis and pay % as the Y-axis. The scatter plot can be reviewed for a number of observations:

1. **Best-Fit Line R^2** – This is the square of the correlation R, which describes how well performance % actually predicts pay %. (Depending on your statistical background, you may seek support in calculating and interpreting these data points.) This correlation, in a strong sales compensation plan, should fall between 60 percent and 90 percent. Higher is better. The more performance measures, formula complexities and plan exceptions that exist in a sales compensation plan, the lower the R^2 tends to be.

2. **Outliers** – You can perform a quick visual scan of each scatter plot to determine which points are problems. These would typically be situations where one incumbent in a sales role performed much lower than others, but received a higher payout, or vice versa. Stories about payouts like this will also make their way through the grapevine at your company and may erode the perception of fairness of the sales compensation plan, and therefore also erode its motivational capacity.

3. **Slope of the Best-Fit Line** – This slope will show, in effect, the average improvement in pay % for every percent increase in Performance. Typically, to deliver motivational upside for individual contributor front-line sales resources, the slope of this line should be just over 1.0.

There is another important piece of analysis to perform with the calculated-field previous-year actual performance percentage. This information for full-year incumbents should be assembled into performance histograms for each role with sufficient population, as illustrated in Figure 5-3 on page 79. These performance curves will tell you three things: whether the goals and territories assigned in the previous year were "fair;" where the excellence point for upside delivery should be going forward (unless territory design; quota allocation or other processes also change significantly); and whether there are any other factors affecting an individual's ability to perform under the sales compensation plan.

As a standard for the first observation, you should expect to see 65 percent of sales professionals meet or exceed their quotas or goals in a given year *when the company hits its overall business plan*. In a normal distribution, you would expect half of the population to be below the "fair" goal (or median) and half above. Due to the human spirit and the motivational nature of the plan/goal combination, you should expect 15 percent more to make the extra effort to get over their goal. Numbers that are lower than 65 percent may reflect a downward economic cycle. If such a cycle does not exist, low numbers would then indicate overaggressive

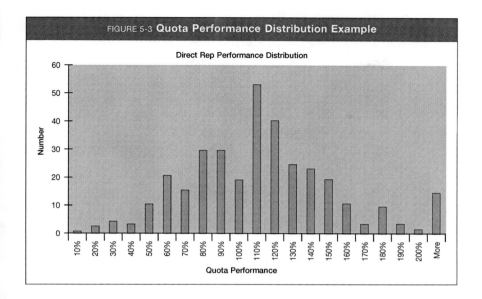

FIGURE 5-3 **Quota Performance Distribution Example**

Direct Rep Performance Distribution

(Chart: Number vs. Quota Performance. Y-axis "Number" from 0 to 60. X-axis "Quota Performance" from 10% to 200% and "More".)

goal-setting or productivity problems due to subpar talent recruitment, sales-process obstacles or products that are not hitting their market demographic with the market-value proposition anticipated. Numbers higher than 65 percent may represent "softball" goals for the salesforce, crediting loopholes or the lack of inclusion of expected new products in the total goal.

The second observation from quota-performance distribution analysis is the appropriate definition of the excellence point for each sales role. Typically, this is the achievement level of the 90th-percentile performer in each role. Many sales organizations establish a compensation philosophy that guides the design of payout formulae so that this 90th-percentile performer is targeted to receive some multiple of target incentive (for example, upside of 2:1 or 3:1). As part of this assessment, you will want to document the amount of upside the 90th-percentile performer actually received under the current plan and performance distribution.

This last observation may require additional analysis. Typically, if the histograms do not appear to be a smooth curve with a slight tail to the right (overachievement) side, there is some additional analysis to understand what is occurring and why. There are standard explanations for certain common phenomena. Bimodal distributions (as illustrated in Figure 5-4 on page 80), with two distinct "humps" of performers, can often indicate two subpopulations within the role that are not treated consistently. For example, senior and junior salesforce members, large accounts and smaller accounts, favored employees and out-of-favor employees. The distributions also can indicate two distinct sales jobs hidden within one title.

It can also be indicative of a selling environment in which there is significant pay at risk, but the sales transactions are large enough for a single transaction to make the difference between 50 percent of quota and 150 percent of quota achievement.

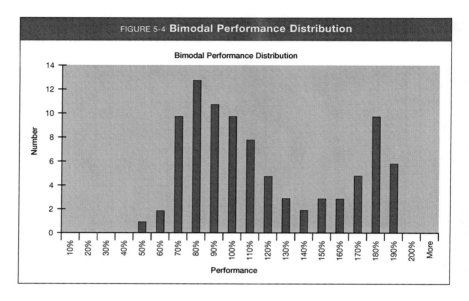

FIGURE 5-4 **Bimodal Performance Distribution**

A slight spin on this data produces yet another analytic with different implications. "Differentiation" analysis takes the pay % numbers for full-year plan participants and stack-ranks them. The analyst then assigns percentiles to each person. These percentiles are divided by the median pay % to display each incumbent, stack-ranked, as a percentage of median actual pay percentage. A graph of this analysis helps portray key observations about upside and downside of the current plans, as illustrated in Figure 5-5 on page 81. Differentiation analysis can be performed-based on variable compensation only, or it can be performed on total cash compensation. The differences will depend on the pay mix for each role.

A final piece of standard analysis derived from internal, historical incumbent pay and performance data is compensation cost of sales analysis. The analyst takes the file of incumbent data and sums the previous-year actual total compensation and then divides this number by the reported revenue for the same organization for the previous year. This will typically yield a number between 1 percent and 10 percent, with most business-to-business companies falling between 4 percent and 8 percent. Companies that come in below 4 percent are often heavily dependent on indirect channels or OEM partnerships to get their products to market.

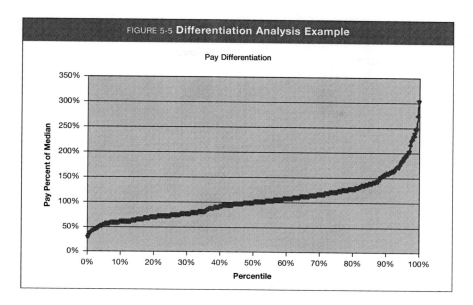

FIGURE 5-5 **Differentiation Analysis Example**

Pay Differentiation

Exceptions arise in the form of large capital-equipment manufacturers who sell directly to extremely large accounts (e.g., a telecom switch manufacturer selling to a carrier or a wafer-fabrication equipment provider selling to semiconductor companies). These types of companies can approach the 1-percent bottom limit.

Conversely, businesses that exceed 8 percent are typically organizations with a complex coverage model and selling processes that require multiple overlay resources to execute a sale. These companies are prime candidates for sales-process reengineering or coverage model redesign if compensation levels cannot be reduced without adversely affecting talent attraction, motivation and retention. A rare company that has established a premium talent strategy in the sales organization may pay much higher than market to attract top talent from competitors, thereby establishing a competitive advantage. These companies typically fund this added expense with higher profit margins than the average industry competitor. Occasionally, this results in incrementally higher sales productivity. Certain industries, like software, skew high on this benchmark as well.

At the same time, the team may also want to sum up all of the previous-year actual revenue credits and assignments from the incumbent data and divide this number by the actual reported revenue from the same organization for the previous year. This will give an overlay factor, or roughly the number of people credited with each dollar of revenue. (A review of Chapter 2's discussion of sales-crediting approaches may be helpful at this point.) The overlay factor counts credit given to territory salesforce members, global-account salesforce members, sales-support resources, telesales, channel managers, multiple layers of sales management and occasionally even customer-service personnel. Multiple crediting is a lightning-rod issue, but few senior executives simplify sales processes to the point necessary to reduce this phenomenon. However, the common alternative of split crediting may create in-fighting, internally focused conversation and administrative difficulties.

External Surveys and Benchmarking Analysis

Market competitiveness is the aspect of sales compensation that receives the most attention, sometimes inappropriately. Almost all companies over a certain size subscribe to compensation surveys. They do so to support an annual compensation-review process (including merit increases, market adjustments, cost-of-living adjustments, etc.) for the entire workforce. A high-quality sales compensation survey can raise the importance and value of the benchmarking exercise to the sales organization.

Benchmarking pay levels and plan practices is an integral part of the sales compensation plan assessment. This analysis will support observations about the competitiveness and appropriateness of target cash compensation (TCC), pay mix, upside and quota size. High-quality sales compensation surveys will also provide important information about job content, geographical indexing and candidate experience to support the sales recruiting and staffing functions that involve HR. The value of these sales compensation surveys, however, is a controversial topic.

There are many survey providers in the market, but not all of them have structured their surveys to provide deep, meaningful information on sales. A worthwhile survey starts with a provider that offers a sales-only survey. It should have 30 or so different types of sales roles, specialized by channel, product, strategy, segment, process focus and level. HR should work with the survey provider to purchase a special cut, populated only with the data of 20 or so comparable companies that are considered direct market or labor competitors. Additionally, if offered, HR should participate in job-matching sessions. These sessions are helpful for your benchmarking process and are likely to improve the quality of the data used in the job-pricing exercise. Surveys that do not include a job-matching session create suspect data at the outset. Similarly, you should pay close attention to the quality of data you submit, because sloppy data submission tends to create a nonproductive atmosphere. You may also want to participate in two to three surveys so that you can triangulate on particularly tricky jobs.

When you have received the survey output, outline your platform jobs and match them to the survey jobs, as applicable. Not all positions will be a strong match, and those that are moderate or weak matches should be noted as such. Focus on channel, management responsibility, sales strategy, account types and years of experience to improve match quality. When matches are weak, the company may choose to fit the role into a particular band that positions it relative to comparable jobs with stronger matches. The analyst should pull TCC, base salary, quota, actual revenue and actual compensation data into the market-pricing model. The analyst should also bracket the specified compensation-benchmarking philosophy of the company. That is, if the company professes to pay at the 60th percentile of the market, the analyst should also pull the data for the 50th and 75th percentiles. As an aside, this stated philosophy should also be derived from a structured discussion of talent scarcity, goal aggressiveness, support provided and other factors deemed critical at your company.

This data should be aged from the effective date of the survey to the current date (aging methodology is often offered in the survey itself; usually a number between 3.5 percent and 4.5 percent is applied per year of aging). The compensation assessment team can then determine the degree to which the company underpays or overpays relative to the market. Before making any recommendations on pay levels, there is a layer of art to place over the scientific analysis conducted to this point. The strategic value of specific roles should be taken into account for the specific company. For example, a telesales role may have a significantly higher strategic value to a company like Dell Computer or Dun & Bradstreet than a company like Kinko's or Caterpillar. That value (or lack of value) can be reflected in a premium or discount to the survey values. Geographical indices can be applied in the same way to provide a national or global framework of sales compensation benchmarks. A completed model (or excerpts) should be supplied to the team.

Sales quotas/goals and actual revenue productivity numbers should be collected, because they are useful data points for making observations about both the effectiveness of a sales compensation plan and the overall fiscal health of the salesforce as a revenue-producing engine.

Some companies will pull 90th-percentile actual compensation data and compare it to the excellence points from their quota-distribution histograms. In situations where a sales role may be new or there is no historical performance data for a job, this piece of benchmark data can be used to shape the upside curve of the formula mechanics.

Qualitative Assessment – Interviews and Surveys

To augment the internal and external quantitative data fed into the sales compensation assessment, many companies will seek qualitative feedback on the sales compensation plans from the field salesforce and executive stakeholders.

These observations are equally important and are especially pertinent to the strategic and role-alignment aspects of the sales compensation assessment. Surveys or interviews can be used for this information-gathering exercise; however, surveys have the benefit of providing statistically significant results from more complete coverage of the organization. The drawback of surveys is the inability of the assessor to probe particular responses and uncover root causes. Ideally, a short survey is supplemented with selected interviews to provide the deepest, richest picture of current sales compensation plan performance.

Developing and deploying an effective internal sales compensation assessment survey (and interviews, for that matter) is not a matter of asking incumbents if they like the plans. The questions for an effective survey must be designed to get at information that is important to the assessor without necessarily revealing the intent to the survey participant. The logical sequence to the survey questions is illustrated in Figure 5-6.

FIGURE 5-6 **Internal Assessment Questions**

1. **Test for understanding of the company strategy and sales strategy** – "How well on a scale of 1-10 do you understand the company's strategy?"
2. **Test for comprehension of the sales compensation plans** – "How well on a scale of 1-10 do you understand your sales compensation plan?" Studies have shown that plan participants who do not understand the plan are rarely motivated by the plan.
3. **Test for comprehension of the goal-development process** – "How well on a scale of 1-10 do you understand the process by which your quota is developed?" This is an indicator of commitment to the goal and is considered a primary driver of the 20-percent productivity uplift that goals provide.
4. **Test for line of sight** – "How much control on a scale of 1-10 do you have over the performance measures included in your plan?"
5. **Test for alignment of the plan with the sales role** – "How well on a scale of 1-10 do you feel your sales compensation plan fits your job responsibilities?"
6. **Test for competitiveness** – "How well on a scale of 1-10 does your sales compensation plan compare to others you have seen for comparable industries and positions?"
7. **Test for differentiation** – "How true on a scale of 1-10 is this statement: If I achieve high levels of performance, I will receive high levels of compensation?" This question can be paired with the quantitative analysis of differentiation to provide additional perspective.
8. **Test for motivation** – "How much motivation on a scale of 1-10 does your sales compensation plan provide?"
9. **Test for confidence in data and administration** – "How confident on a scale of 1-10 are you that the data used to calculate your sales compensation is accurate?" We typically see a drop-off in motivation as accuracy of sales compensation data drops below the low- to mid-90-percent range.
10. **Test for results** – "How often on a scale of 1-10 has the sales compensation plan encouraged you to perform at a higher level?"
11. **Test for satisfaction** – "How satisfied on a scale of 1-10 are you with your current sales compensation plan?"
12. **Test for retention** – "If you were ever to leave this company, how much of a contributor to your departure would sales compensation be on a scale of 1-10?"

Solicit additional qualitative feedback – *"What other issues do you have with the sales compensation plans?"*

The results of this kind of survey provide insight and validation to the assessment process (especially if there were hypotheses or political agendas leaning toward certain preconceived solutions in the first implementation). This survey becomes a truly useful tool when conducted in a consistent manner in consecutive years to provide trend analysis and validation of change-management initiatives.

Executive interviews build upon this approach to provide deeper insight into the organizational underpinnings of the salesforce. As part of the strategic alignment aspect of sales compensation plan assessment, executive interviews should delve into the following topics:

- What are the goals of the company for the next year? The sales organization?
- How does the structure of the organization support these goals?
- What products will be emphasized in the upcoming periods?
- What customers offer the most potential?
- What buying criteria are most important?
- What parts of the sales process are most important in delivering value to the customer and executing the strategy of the organization?
- What sales roles are the most important to successfully execute the sales strategy?
- Is the organization able to recruit sufficient talent to succeed? Which sales roles are the most difficult to recruit?
- How well does the current sales compensation plan support the company's initiatives?
- What issues exist with the sales compensation plan?

Administrative Assessment

An assessment of administrative practices and processes associated with the sales compensation plan is important for understanding how effectively the plan is performing. In many organizations, this is a frequently ignored piece of assessment. However, unless members of the salesforce are paid correctly and on time, the plan loses the ability to motivate and reward successfully.

Key factors to review include the following:

- Administrative responsibilities: Are they clearly defined and adhered to?
- Administrative systems: For each performance measure, where is the data tracked, measured and reported?
- Payout: Are there numerous requests for exceptions? Are issues uncovered frequently about the accuracy of payouts? Are payouts made on time?

Tools that help this part of the assessment include data-flow charts, as available through IT, and in-depth interviews with those personnel involved in all aspects of sales compensation administration. In addition, it's likely that you and your team will have gained valuable insights into the efficiency and accuracy of administration through the interviews or surveys you have completed with the sales organization. As a byproduct of this assessment, you should be able to document the administrative processes if they have not already been explicitly recorded.

Summing Up

You will collect several kinds of findings in the assessment process. Because both data analysis and qualitative assessment tasks have provided the information used in the assessment, the team will have findings that reflect both the perceptions and actual practices that exist in the organization. Qualitatively, the team will be able to determine if the plan supports the company's strategic plan, and whether appropriate emphasis has been placed on measures and approaches that are consistent with each role's strategic impact. Findings will also provide the team with information on the extent to which the plans reward the selling behaviors required, or if intended/undesirable behaviors have occurred.

Rigorous data analysis will verify the degree to which pay levels, productivity expectations and practices are competitive. Data will also be available to answer questions about cost of sales and the degree to which required top-line and bottom-line results are being achieved. Finally, the team will know if plans are being paid out accurately and on time, or if there is an acceptable number of exceptions and issues.

Successful completion of a thorough assessment process is a critical element in the design process. It provides the design team with the information needed to ensure that any negative aspects of the current plan can be addressed so that they are not repeated in a new or redesigned plan.

chapter 6

DESIGNING A NEW SALES COMPENSATION PLAN

VI

Designing a new sales compensation plan, or just tweaking the old one, means that the plan your company currently uses will be changed. This is a critically important concept, because when a company designs and implements a new sales compensation plan, it means not only that the plan will change, but that some members of the salesforce may earn more and some may earn less based on their results. Before implementing the process of plan design or redesign, it is essential for management to support the possibility and direction of change. Also, the design team and you, as the HR professional, must be knowledgeable about the current plan and its supporting programs, based on the assessment work described in Chapter 5. It is critical to be aware of both the degree of change that is required and acceptable to your company. This is especially the case because your solicitation of feedback on the plan will create organizational expectations of future change or action.

The following sections in this chapter will help you understand some of the business drivers of potential change and guide you through the plan-design process:

- Preparing for the New Plan-Design Process
- Defining Sales Compensation Plan Change Objectives
- Building Plan Designs
- Costing the New Sales Compensation Plan Design
- Types of Costing Analyses.

The chapter also includes a discussion of aspects of your sales compensation plan that might change and the degree of possible alterations, and provides guidance designed to ensure that the recommended changes have the desired business impact while remaining within the range of management tolerance for change.

Preparing for the New Plan-Design Process
The optimal plan-design process was explained in Chapter 4. As indicated in both Chapters 1 and 4, the HR professional may serve in many different roles relative

to this process. Preparation for any of the roles described requires that you fully understand your company's sales compensation plan as well as the practices and terminology related to the sales process and sales jobs that your company uses. Although this book presents terminology and generally accepted principles that are technically correct, both vocabulary and practice may be different at your company. Taking the time to learn how your company thinks and talks about sales programs and practices will give you a stronger professional presence at the table during the sales compensation design process.

Whether your role in the design team is process leader, subject-matter expert or team member, you will also need to ensure that an effective assessment of the current plan has been completed. As discussed in Chapter 5, the assessment should be based on business objectives and issues identified throughout the plan year. These issues should guide the development of a preferred approach for your formal sales compensation plan evaluation – both quantitative and qualitative. The assessment will provide you with data, observations and potential issues for the sales compensation design team to address. Each component of the assessment will help you to answer critical questions related to plan change, such as the following:

1. What behaviors, actions or results do we want the plan to reward (or drive) or continue to reward or drive?
2. What behaviors, actions or results do we not want the plan to reward (or drive) or to discontinue rewarding?
3. Are these consistent with the job roles we have in place?
4. Is our pay competitive with the market for the talent we need?
5. Does the data help us understand the potential impact of continuing with the current plan or changing the plan design?
6. Can the possible changes be cost-effectively administered?

The results of the assessment should be presented to the design team and ultimately to management for its support of plan change objectives. As an HR representative, you should develop your own understanding of the answers to these questions and provide support in the evaluation process to ensure that it is providing the team and management with an understanding of the current situation and requirements of the plan, regardless of your role in plan design.

Defining Sales Compensation Plan Change Objectives

The plan has been assessed, and you or other members of the team have talked with senior management about what is needed for next year. As described in Chapter 4, the first key step in any design process is the development of plan objectives. It is critical to agree on why change is needed and why it's needed now.

Requirements for a change in the sales compensation plan can be the result of several factors, including the following:

- Talent acquisition and retention (for example, your company experiences high levels of voluntary turnover, or you have difficulty hiring qualified talent)
- Technical issues with design (for example, things you learned during your quantitative assessment that suggest that the plan is not structured to support key selling objectives)
- Organizational biases (for example, differing management agendas or objectives for directing the salesforce through the compensation plan).

While these issues need to be addressed, perhaps the most significant and overriding reason to alter the plan is a change in the strategic direction of the business.

The Impact of Sales and Business Changes on Sales Compensation Success
Because sales compensation should support the achievement of a sales organization's strategies and objectives, a change in your selling environment or a change in your business direction should cause you to evaluate if your plan still supports the required results you seek from your salesforce. This section provides an overview of six major change factors as well as implications for sales compensation design, particularly related to selecting performance measures and allocating the financial quota or quotas used in the plan.

1. New Products. New products, whether they are line extensions or entirely new, can have significant impact on the productivity of your salesforce. First, with these products come some expectation of sales results, and thus a typical increase of the total objectives of the salesforce. However, that increase must take into account the possible cannibalization of existing products or the possibility that existing products won't sell because of anticipation for the new product. Second, the salesforce must be comfortable with the features, benefits and impact of the new product on its customers and may require time to prepare new sales approaches for the new products.

Key issues that must be addressed as you plan for total and product-specific results (and thus, the performance measures and productivity expectations reflected in the sales compensation plan) include: (1) The time and effort to assimilate the new products and to sell them may displace time spent on existing products so that new product sales may not be totally incremental; and (2) A different sales approach for the new products, either a longer sales cycle and/or a focus on additional or separate buyers within the accounts. Therefore, the organization must again assess the impact of these requirements on total and product-specific productivity.

If new products are dramatically different in their required sales approach, the company should determine if special emphasis should be placed on new product sales achievement. It should do this by carving out either part of the at-risk pay for those products or by enhancing upside within the plan for achievement of new product sales.

2. New Types of Transactions. New types of transactions indicate a change in the way a sale might occur. These can include a shift from a one-time invoice and payment to annual payments over time to actually providing leasing or financing of the purchase. This change in transaction type means the value of the sales signed in total may be less or more than is currently recognized as revenue or sales credit for the purposes of sales compensation calculation. This situation may be the case for different products or for some types of initial transactions before a full deal closes (such as a product trial or a technical assessment). In such a circumstance, the company must determine if it wants to motivate or reward different types of transactions or to treat all transactions the same. Either decision should be reflected in sales crediting rules and in the measures used in the sales compensation plan.

3. Competition or Competitive Action. Competitive new products, alliances or even deep price discounting can require a product and sales management reaction to the competitive event, which may result in the need to address the situation in the sales compensation plan. Many companies learn that the need to increase discounts to compete effectively can actually create erosion in a revenue base and create a stronger burden on achieving each salesforce member's objectives. This means that practices such as aggressive thresholds (for example, an account manager might have to surpass the past year's sales to receive payout) or a component based on price realization or margin-percent achievement may punish salesforce members for a market condition and could lead to demoralization, turnover or both. Therefore, using these kinds of measures in the sales compensation plan should be considered carefully and tested against realistic achievement scenarios if there is agreement that they could support achievement of the company's objectives.

4. Degree of Growth/Profitability Required. A successful sales compensation plan starts with an achievable set of sales objectives. Many a head of sales has pushed back when the CEO promises double the market growth rate or significant increases in gross margin without the products and market differential to support the outcome. This is sometimes seen when companies build "stretch" objectives into the quotas allocated but not into the business plan. This in essence results in a reduction in earnings for the salesforce, because sales objectives are unachievable. However, if significant but achievable stretch is built into the objectives, the result should be additional pay/upside for the salesforce, not a reduction. Any significant change in the overall objectives requires sales management to support the change and be able to make the case for how results can be accomplished. Management should also ensure that it is held to the same numbers.

5. Mergers, Acquisitions and Spinoffs. Even the companies touted as the best at managing business combinations or divestitures often fail to think through the sales implications of these changes. These business combinations result in the addition or elimination of potential customer segments or buyers as well as the expansion or contraction of products/services within the portfolio available to the salesforce to sell. First and foremost in this arena, there is a need for transition periods. Companies in these situations seek to ensure consistency and support for the transaction. Mutual sales coverage and the need for sales-teaming must be assessed. Some members of the salesforce may move from a lead sales role to sales support or specialist depending on the situation. In such cases, team objectives and/or cross-sell incentive plans may be justified. Alternatively, some members of the salesforce may lose products to sell, be reassigned or worse, have pay reduced. In the latter case, the scarcity of talent and its impact on total results must be considered as you develop the ultimate coverage model and related sales compensation plans and transition strategies.

6. New Partners or Third-Party Channels for Selling or Fulfillment. Companies looking to develop efficiencies in sales coverage and fulfillment often look toward third parties or channel partners to provide representation or complete some steps within the sales-service continuum. Typically, these third parties have existing relationships within the market the company is targeting or have experience in executing the fulfillment activities. They may even be involved in some aspect of assembly or packaging. Examples of these types of third parties are agents, resellers, distributors and assembly or subassembly/contract-manufacturing organizations.

In some cases, these relationships are intended to displace current sales activity. In other cases, they are intended to allow the seller more sales leverage and extended coverage. In displacement, the key issue is the reassignment of customers away from the direct seller to the third party and the assignment of a role to manage the partner relationship. In the leverage model, the most significant issue is question of crediting and data availability. The concern here is whether the salesforce member gets full or partial credit for these sales (third-party sales often are at lower prices in order to allow the third party some margin) and whether a third party will provide data that tracks sales volume to the customers with whom the direct seller still maintains relationships. To resolve crediting issues, it is important to determine at the outset if management expects the utilization of new channels to drive down sales compensation costs.

Plan-Change Objectives

Once the primary drivers for change have been identified, you and the design team will be able to define plan change objectives. Plan-change objectives are statements of the business impact the company is attempting to achieve. The sales compensation plan must support the objectives, which can include the following:

- Drive the achievement of new product revenue.
- Ensure channel neutrality that allows customers to buy through their desired sources.
- Reinforce profitable selling.
- Ensure the retention of top-achieving talent.
- Provide overall cost neutrality, except for higher results.
- Attract top talent to open positions.

As a participant in the plan-design process, your goal is to identify both pay implications that may result from these change objectives and alternative approaches to addressing those implications. The alternatives can be presented to the steering committee for a test of whether it is really ready to accept the type of change implied by the objectives. In some cases, the plan change may have some implications for sales coverage/job design, total costs, administrative processes, systems requirements and reporting that are either unachievable or that may require additional cross-functional input. In these cases, management may seek to evaluate the decision-making and approval process for plan change to ensure that the appropriate input is in place before it provides commitment to and approval of the plan changes.

Building Plan Designs

In Chapters 4 and 5, we identified a preferred approach for the design team to follow and the possible implications of short-circuiting that process. This section describes the following components that can be used when you are working on a change in plan design:

- Eligibility
- Target Cash Compensation (TCC)
- Incentive Mix and Upside
- Sales Credit
- Performance Measures
- Measurement and Payment Cycles
- Plan Types and Incentive Formulas.

It is important for the plan-design team to consider each component, the degree of change that is required and acceptable, and the indicators that suggest a need to move from your current plan in a certain direction.

Eligibility. CEOs and other senior managers increasingly indicate that it is the responsibility of all employees having contact with customers to help the company grow revenues. The practical reality, however, is that not all employees are in a position to influence customer-buying decisions. This fact raises the question of how to determine the jobs that should be eligible to participate in the sales compensation plan. Before embarking on a plan redesign, the positions eligible for participation in the plan should be confirmed. Companies typically use at least three criteria for establishing or confirming eligibility for participation, as described in Chapter 2:

1. The primary responsibility of employees in designated sales jobs is customer contact and persuading the customer to do business with the company.

2. Employees can affect sales results and may have assigned sales goals.

3. Sales results can be tracked and accurately measured at the employee level.

In general, it is these requirements that are used to identify the jobs that should be eligible for a sales compensation plan. While there are often other jobs that have customer-contact responsibility – for example, customer-service representative jobs – unless the job meets the criteria, it should not be eligible for participation in the sales compensation plan.

Target Cash Compensation (TCC). TCC represents the amount of cash compensation provided to a sales job for the accomplishment of target performance. Again, target performance can be based on individual quota or on average productivity requirements of similar sales roles within an organization. As noted previously, TCC can take many formats. The key consideration relevant to change is the degree to which your company is providing a pay package that will attract, motivate and retain the caliber of talent needed to achieve your sales objectives. Primary indicators of a need to address TCC are turnover and performance.

Too much turnover, especially of new hires and top performers, implies that there is not enough compensation available within the pay plan. Too much turnover may also be indicative of other plan-design issues, but the key to knowing if the problem is caused by too little TCC is if the company can recruit quality talent to replace the lost talent. If it can attract new talent, the package is attractive and the answer lies elsewhere in the employee value proposition (EVP).

The other reason for considering TCC change is whether your company has the talent to achieve the sales results required. If your sales organization has low turnover but is not able to achieve objectives (either total volume or other strategic objectives), it is possible that the TCC is too low to attract the quality of talent needed. In such a circumstance, you would need to upgrade your salesforce, and increasing TCC would be a critical part of that effort.

Increasing TCC for existing populations is not an automatic fix for talent-management issues. While funding is likely to be a potential issue, you'll find that more money does not necessarily increase current talent levels. Most companies start by restating the desired range of TCC to attract and retain the appropriate talent. Restating the range does not mean changing individual pay levels. Instead, companies should ask the sales management team to rank-order performers based on skills and achievement, both current and expected future potential. The total salesforce should then be evaluated individually to determine which employees get increases and which stay at their current level. Staying at the current level may appear inequitable, but in fact the approach is consistent with a pay-for-performance culture. Thus, companies should establish new standards and put the salesforce on a performance plan with the awareness of the fact that they now have new TCC ranges with which to hire new talent.

While changing TCC is a straightforward approach, when companies are paying too low (either at target or at upside), sales management is often afraid to manage out-par or subpar performers. The reason for this is that the absence of a salesforce member (and therefore the presence of an undercovered territory or accounts) when management is trying to hit its numbers limits its ability to do so more than carrying a moderate performer, because it is not guaranteed that a new and better performer can be hired. In such a scenario, the result is often a cycle of non-performance.

If a company determines that it is in fact overpaying, the problem is typically handled by either increasing average quotas or targets or by establishing new pay levels for new hires. Over time, pay is managed down to cost-effective levels, and any talent beyond that of the company's current requirements either is moved into management or moves itself out of the organization. The key lesson here is that dramatic changes in compensation levels should rarely be applied across the board and should be implemented over time.

Incentive Mix and Upside. Incentive mix represents the ratio between base salary and target-incentive compensation as a percentage of TCC. Upside represents the amount of pay provided to top performers and is typically expressed as a ratio of the number of dollars of overtarget earnings the company will provide for each dollar of at-risk incentive. (See Chapter 2, Figure 2-5.)

Incentive mix and upside do not need to exactly match the market; however, you do need to be able to sell your mix and top earnings opportunities to recruits and current employees being faced with competitive offers from other firms. The following approaches (and their indicators) may be useful when considering changing mix:

1. Increasing Incentive Mix – "Putting more money at risk." An example would be taking an account manager from a 70/30 plan with a 2:1 upside (resulting in total payout of 160 percent of TCC for top earners) to a 60/40 plan with a 2:1 upside (resulting in total payout of 180 percent of TCC). This would be what some managers call "getting more skin in the game." Indicators of this need would arise from the following comments or symptoms:

- Members of the salesforce appear too complacent about hitting their numbers.
- Members of the salesforce complain that there is not enough earnings differentiation between top performers and par performers.
- Members of the salesforce are reluctant to focus on a certain part of the plan.
- Managers feel that the salesforce starts sandbagging (holding back) sales toward the end of a performance period.
- Top performers are leaving for competitors who offer higher total-earnings opportunities.

Typically, these factors should be tested. But should you choose to move in this direction, you have some decisions to make. First, do you make the change all in one period or over multiple performance periods? A change of up to 10 percent can typically be handled in a single period. Second, you must ask if you are willing to reduce salary. In many companies, lowering salary is "taboo." Whether or not you choose to change salaries, you should at least make sure that you do not increase them through a merit process only to later reverse the process in order to shift the balance. Holding back merits for one or two periods and putting dollars into the target incentive is one way of moving toward the desired outcome. Another approach is to transition through a guarantee to the old salary but force the seller to re-earn those dollars during the period. If you do this, their sales results will need to produce payouts up to the old salary value before they receive any additional dollars. In this case, the salary is reduced, but the salesforce is generally given a separate monthly check for the difference, and incentive earnings are netted against that amount before they are disbursed. Such a transition requires only one performance period.

To ensure that upside is increased for top performers, the acceleration rate must be applied to new total-target incentives; thus a larger dollar amount is being accelerated. Getting more dollars to top performers can also be accomplished by increasing the acceleration for those truly in the top tier of performance. With the increased risk, you'll have some funding to support this action.

2. Decreasing Incentive Mix – "Putting more money in salary." In this example, you might take an account manager from a 50/50 plan with a 2:1 upside to a 70/30 plan with a 2:1 upside. Indicators of this need include the following:

- Some sales roles may be teamed, with little control over total sales results.
- You are losing talent to companies offering higher salaries.
- Some members of the salesforce are not spending enough time on deals with a longer sales cycle for fear of being short of cash in the current period.
- Members of the salesforce move off of opportunities too quickly and excessively rely on post-sales to complete the deal.
- The amount of earnings of top performers seems to cause payouts that are too rich and may not be cost-effective.

Shifting to a reduced risk is clearly easier, because you are increasing security for members of the salesforce. But you are also sending a message to top performers that they may have some earnings limitation (less upside). Additionally, you may be sending a message to lower performers that they can relax. With a reduced risk, it is generally best to readdress the topic of TCC in order to ensure that you've got your better players in the higher ranges of pay. You should not be afraid to reduce TCC for those who should also be put on performance-plan evaluation status.

From a cost perspective, reducing TCC for selected members of the salesforce may reduce the variability of costs, but it also puts more pressure on fixed costs. The total effect should be modeled so that you can achieve the right balance for the entire group.

Sales Credit. Sales-credit policies and procedures are essential to the success of a sales compensation plan. Specifically, sales credit represents the point in time at which a salesforce member is given credit and the amount of credit received for a specific transaction. The goal of credit timing is to balance the proximity of the activities and results leading to the transaction with the need to ensure the salesforce member remains engaged throughout the customer relationship. Classically, most companies provide sales credit for transactions either at the time the order is booked or closed (thus providing closeness to a customer's buying decision) or at the time of invoicing (also referred to as *shipment*), which is when the transaction becomes financially an asset (that is, revenue and a receivable) of the company. Some companies will split sales credit between these two events (booking and shipment or booking and revenue recognition) when the time between them is significantly long. Other companies, although very few, provide total or partial crediting at the time the customer actually pays for the products or services. Those companies paying on collection support their actions by saying it helps the company balance cash flow, but highly experienced compensation plan designers believe it to be a poor balancing method because it puts the onus on the salesforce. In fact, it may actually take the salesforce away from selling and motivate them to function as collections agents!

Sales-crediting challenges and changes occur most often when the company experiences changes in products, transactions or sales-channel partners. An example of such a change is selling multiple-year deals that are either prepaid or paid annually. Similarly, issues occur when a company provides a pre-transaction service such as a proof of concept. A payment is made for that service, but there is not a guarantee that the traditional deal will occur. Lastly, these issues arise when multiple sellers touch a transaction, such as when a headquarters salesforce member works with buyers, but the sale is delivered to a site in a separate location and is covered by a second geography-salesforce member, or when the sale is delivered by a channel partner who is covered by a channel-account manager.

The most critical aspect of changing sales crediting based on these types of changes is ensuring that the credit supports the desired selling efforts and results. Split crediting (for example, 50 percent to the headquarters salesforce member, 25 percent to the geography-salesforce member and 25 percent to the channel-account manager) often results in decreased cooperation in a complex selling model. The result can be unintended behaviors such as not communicating with the geography-salesforce member or discounting to undercut the channel partner and thus the account manager. Providing 100-percent credit to all players can create that cooperation, but it also creates (in the just-mentioned example) as much as 300-percent crediting to the sales team. This fact implies that either a lower commission rate must be paid for the deals in order to make them affordable or that these deals and crediting must be built into the overall quota allocation and then later removed from revenue recognition to ensure financial results are in line with sales results.

Changes to crediting require significant upfront timing for testing of administrative, reporting and other operational aspects of the plan. Further, they require significant communications and financial modeling to sell to the field and to senior executives within your organization.

Performance Measures. As discussed in previous chapters, most plans should contain no more than three performance measures. A sales volume or production measure is typically assigned the primary performance weight in the plan. It is often assigned a weight of 60 percent or more. The remaining 40 percent weight is distributed between the other two measures, but no measure should have a weight of less than 15 percent. A lower weight dilutes the motivational impact of the measure.

In a plan change, measures may be added or removed. The latter is perhaps the more difficult of the two. If plans for your salesforce have four or more components, you should consider reducing the number and ensuring that there is sufficient focus on the sales volume component. This means that your company needs to rely on total performance management and sales manager effectiveness to support those other measures, not variable compensation. However, removing a measure can create concern, particularly if payout for the component has been on or above target, or if the measure has been in place for several plan generations. Adding measures or components represents the most typical change to an existing sales compensation plan. This change is usually reflective of a change in sales focus or strategic direction, such as new products, new customers or better profitability.

Two key considerations should be taken into account when introducing an additional measure or component. First, the measure and its weighting should not detract from the overall results desired (typically, total volume achievement). To ensure this does not occur, the weighting of the component and the ability to overearn on it should be limited to 30 percent (and can be less if there is a large amount of pay at risk or if the design is linked to total volume). The weighting can also affect the cash flow of the individual salesforce members if the component is not paid as frequently as the one it is replacing. Second, the data must be easily available, well-understood and auditable. In addition, the range of potential performance must be relatively stable. Untested measurements in a new plan are the most common causes for its failure (and the necessary reversion to the prior plan). A conservative rule of thumb is that a new measure should be tracked for six months (to validate accuracy and timely availability) before the organization uses it for compensation. Salesforce members and sales managers who do not trust the data or the fairness of the new component will be very vocal about the possible impact on their time and any perceptions they have about the inequities in the plan. Inequities must be caught early and addressed effectively in order to save any new measurement and restore salesforce morale.

Measurements and Payment Cycles. These cycles represent the period of time over which performance is measured for one or more plan components and how frequently there is some interim payout in advance of the close of the cycle. Once developed, they are the least likely components to change within an existing plan. The exceptions occur if there are preceding changes to incentive mix and/or to plan measurements and components.

The design team should ask if increased or decreased incentive mix and upside would result in significant changes to cash flow or whether the payout amounts are too big or too small to have the desired effect. Increasing the payout cycle length (resulting in less-frequent payouts) assumes that the average payout in the new plan will be larger and thus have more impact. Decreasing the payout cycle (and thus increasing the frequency of payout) implies smaller payouts and might be considered where waiting too long for cash might cause undesired cash-flow strain. For example, a shift in mix to 60/40 from 80/20 might imply you need to change payouts from quarterly to monthly. Figure 6-1 presents guidelines relative to these cycles.

FIGURE 6-1 Impact of Mix on Payout Cycle/Frequency				
Incentive Mix	<= 25/75	30/70 – 65/35	70/30 – 80/20	85/15 – 100/+
Prescribed Payout Cycle	Weekly or Monthly	Monthly	Monthly or Quarterly	Quarterly or Annually

Plan Types and Incentive Formulas. As described in Chapter 2, there are two basic types of sales incentive plans: commission and bonus. Some companies will use both in the same plan, thus implementing a *combination plan*. However, regardless of the type of plan a company uses to pay its salesforce, many companies find that it is useful to maintain the same type of plan year over year. However, they might adjust or tweak the incentive rates within the plan formulas to reflect the need for a change in sales focus.

Both the use of plan types and the incentive formula mechanics have a predictable pattern of change that is related to how a company grows and matures in its business. That pattern can be described as "generational;" that is, moving from one level of sales compensation plan sophistication to the next based on the depth and breadth of the organization's product portfolio, the markets/customers served and management's focus for the business.

The successive generations of sales compensations plans, particularly the incentive plan arrangement, can be described as follows:

First Generation – Commission plan for all sales resources, both sellers and their managers. The business rationale is relatively simple and straightforward: All business is good business.

Second Generation – Ramped (or "tiered") commission plan with accelerator based on total volume or products' volume. The business rationale: More business is good business.

Third Generation – Commission plan plus some simple bonus. As the company begins to mature through the introduction of product-line extension, new products or both, one or more bonuses may be added to the incentive plan in order to direct strategic selling. The business rationale is: Some kinds of business are more valuable than others.

Fourth Generation – Quota-based bonus for managers, commission plan with bonuses for sellers. A realization that field sales managers need to be more strategic in their roles and actions related to the business sets in at this level. While the salesforce's incentive plan may be continued from the third generation, the managers' plan shifts in focus from being largely a reflection of the salesforce's plan to being one that includes more strategic measures. Such measures may include focus on sales profitability, expense management and sales productivity (for example, the number of members of the salesforce who meet or exceed their assigned sales quota). The business rationale is: Only certain business is good business, and to achieve this realization, front-line managers must be more proactive in managing for profitability and productivity.

Fifth Generation – Quota-based bonus plan for all. Ultimately, companies come to the realization that there is a need for alignment throughout the sales organization. This alignment is achieved through the implementation of quota-based bonus plans (for all salesforce and sales management positions) that are based on increased knowledge of the company's markets and the resident potential in accounts and territories. The business rationale is: Top-to-bottom alignment to optimize achievement of only certain business is good business.

As with any conceptual guideline, companies may move faster or slower through this progression based on changes in their markets, competition and their own management maturity. While some may begin with a quota-based bonus for all roles, and some may never move beyond a ramped commission plan, the important point is that plans must fit with what senior management is striving to accomplish with the business at a particular point in time. There will occasionally be emotional attachment (or rejection) of specific mathematical formulas. If, as a design team, you cannot get around these blockages, rest assured that there is another mathematical method to arrive at your desired state that will not require you to use terminology with "baggage." There are, however, some common objectives in terms of what is important to the business and what an incentive plan design that addresses those objectives might look like.

Illustrative plan designs that address the most common objectives of a company when changing its sales compensation plan include the following:

- How to incent balanced product-line selling (Figure 6-2, page 103)
- How to incent profitable selling (Figure 6-3, page 104)

- How to incent new product selling (Figure 6- 4, page 104)
- How to incent sales managers to improve the sales performance of all territories so that there is an incentive to fill all territories and develop members of the salesforce (Figure 6- 5, page 105).

FIGURE 6-2 **Incentive Plan Illustration – Incenting Balanced Product-Line Selling**

- Target Total Compensation: $100,000
- Mix: 60% / 40%
- Salary Range Midpoint: $ 60,000
- Target Incentive Amount: $ 40,000

Plan Component	Weight	Value
Total Sales vs. Quota	80%	$32,000
Product Mix Multiplier	20%	$8,000

Total Sales vs Quota Bonus
(Rate per point, or dollar value of each 1 percent achieved)

1% – 100% of quota	$320 per percent achieved
Over 100%	$640 for each additional percent achieved

Product Mix Multiplier (Based on Number of Product Quotas Achieved)
(Additional incentive paid as percent of total bonus earned year-to-date.)

Number of Product Quotas	Percent Bonus (Times Total Bonuses Earned)
5 of 5	75%
4 of 5	50%
3 of 5	25%
2 of 5	15%
1 of 5	0%

Whatever the change, analyses on cost and earnings impact must be completed. As mentioned earlier, the company must ensure that the new plan measurements and components are well-understood and that potential volatility is managed. Techniques for managing the predictability of payout in aggressive sales compensation environments include the following:

1. Establish a separate payout with an easy entry level or threshold but a limited or capped payout.

2. Establish a second payout, but ensure it only occurs if the salesforce member overachieves a specified gate or hurdle (for example, 95 percent total quota achievement) before any payout is provided. Such a technique might also include some cap or limited top-end payout for the component.

FIGURE 6-3 Incentive Plan Illustration – Incenting Profitable Selling (Sales Rep)

- Target Total Compensation: $100,000
- Mix: 60% / 40%
- Salary Range Midpoint: $60,000
- Target Incentive Amount: $40,000

Plan Component	Weight	Value
Revenue vs. Quota	100%	$40,000
Gross-Margin Hurdle	If the Gross-Margin Hurdle of 20% is achieved, then payout at or above the 51% revenue commission rate is available. Otherwise, the payout rate remains at 2.0%.	

Revenue Commission

Percent of Quotas	Rate
0% – 50%	2.0%
51% – 100%	4.0%
101% – 125%	6.0%
126% and greater	8.0%

FIGURE 6-4 Incentive Plan Illustration — Incenting New Product Selling

- Target Total Compensation: $100,000
- Mix: 60% / 40%
- Salary Range Midpoint: $60,000
- Target Incentive Amount: $40,000

Plan Component	Weight	Value
Total Volume vs. Quota	75%	$30,000
Product-Launch Commission	25%	$10,000

Total Volume vs. Quota Bonus

Percent of Quota Achieved	Annual Payout Per %
1% – 100%	$300
Above 100%	$600

Product-Launch Commission

Volume to $100,000	10%
Volume over $100,000	15%

- Target Total Compensation: $100,000
- Mix: 60% / 40%
- Salary Range Midpoint: $60,000
- Target Incentive Amount: $40,000

Plan Component	Weight	Value
Region Revenue vs. Quota	75%	$30,000
Performance of Territories	25%	$10,000

Region Revenue vs. Quota Bonus

Percent of Quota Achieved	Payout Rate Per Percent Achieved
0% – 75%	$ 0
76% – 100%	$ 1,200
101% – 110%	$ 2,250
111% and greater	$ 2,400

Performance of Territories (assume 12 territories)

Territories @ or > Plan	Annual Payout
4 or fewer territories	$ 0
5 – 6 territories	$ 5,000
7 – 10 territories	$10,000*
11 – 12 territories	$15,000

*Target achievement

3. Promote the second measure so that it only goes to those who achieve total quotas by utilizing one plan accelerator (overquota rate) for achievement over 100 percent but a higher plan accelerator for being above 100 percent and achieving the target amount of the second measure. Doing this ensures the best payouts go to those who have done both, but strongly links the total payout to the achievement of total quota.

Costing the New Sales Compensation Plan Design

If designing a new sales compensation plan is a combination of behavioral, strategic and financial architecture, *costing* the new design is half the battle. While HR and sales are often given the lead in the behavioral aspect (due to experience in behavioral science and a more detailed knowledge of exactly which behaviors are desired, respectively), that is rarely the case for the cost-analysis and budgetary projections for the proposed plan design. While finance will often have this responsibility, it is important that HR and sales be fluent in the structure and language of the process. All who are involved in the design, review and administration of the sales compensation plan should understand the cost drivers, key assumptions and relative benchmarks.

The cost drivers for sales compensation are more complex than they appear at first glance. If compensation cost of selling (CCOS) is an ultimate performance metric for a sales compensation plan, it is a logical exercise to break down the drivers. Actual cash compensation cost for eligible sales resources is the numerator. As the numerator goes up, CCOS increases. The denominator in the calculation of CCOS is revenue. As the denominator goes down, CCOS increases. See Figure 6-6 for factors that can drive CCOS.

FIGURE 6-6 **Factors Affecting CCOS as a Percent of Revenue**	
Factors Affecting Driving Up Actual CCOS	**Factors Affecting Decreasing Revenue**
• "Inclusive" eligibility (although this is really just moving costs around, into and out of the sales function) • TCC pay levels • Overall headcount • Performance levels and productivity expectations • Pay mix (in an overachieving organization) • Plan upside or acceleration • Standard deviation of performance distribution (breadth of performance in an accelerated or ramped plan) • Shift of transactions to or from direct channels • Credit duplication if not allowed for in quota allocation • Design mistakes, unintended loopholes or fraud	• Extending the sales cycle • Increases in workload • Reduction of time allocated to selling activities • Employee turnover (due to uncovered accounts and productivity ramp for new resources) • Reduction in transaction size • Decrease in average account size • Decrease in close rates • Decrease in lead flow • Decrease in product availability

Not all potential factors need to be included in sales compensation plan cost modeling. Some companies use only headcount times target-pay level. Most include some assumption of different levels of performance. The important thing is to recognize that you are in essence stating, "We assume all of these things will remain the same next year" when you choose not to include factors.

Assumptions are a fact of life when cost-modeling sales compensation. No one should expect to foresee the future with 100-percent accuracy. You do, however, want to equip the steering committee and the salesforce with the ability to make the most intelligent managerial decisions possible in the approval and administration of the plan. Several of the factors listed would not be assumptions, because they would have been explicitly included in the design decisions themselves (pay levels, pay mix, accelerators, etc.). These drivers are design factors that can be revisited should the forecasted cost of the proposed plan exceed budgets/constraints.

Many of the other factors may be assumptions that should be documented in the cost analysis. For example, if you assume that bundling a new product into proposed solutions will increase both the close rate and transaction size, and this assumed increase is included in the quotas assigned, you would expect that CCOS would come down. Revenue would increase, but achievement should not. The numerator stays flat and the denominator goes up. If costing of the plan then returns a CCOS higher than the previous year's, the design team should investigate what other factors counteracted the assumed increase in productivity. The goal is completeness of the analysis, but you will need to recognize when you have passed a point of declining returns on your cost-analysis effort.

If the current plan assessment included a complete quantitative analysis, it will be useful to retain the spreadsheets supporting that work for the costing of the new sales compensation plan. One of the most popular methodologies for plan-cost comparison takes the assessment's current list of incumbents and actual distributions of performance and applies them against the new pay levels, new pay mixes and new pay formulas. This method provides a cost analysis that is very good for an "apples-to-apples" comparison of the new plan relative to the previous year, but may not be exact for budgeting (if headcount goes up or down the following year, for example, you will need to understand how many, what types, the composition of their offer packages and what productivity to expect from any new hires).

Types of Costing Analyses

This section describes three key cost analyses:

- Change in Total Cost
- Change in Individual Earnings
- Total Cost Compared to Budget.

Change in Total Cost. This change looks at the total projected cost of the new plan for the same people that were on the plan in the previous year. In this analysis, any differences are due to changes in TCC, mix and upside, and other tools implemented within the plan design. These include hurdles, gates, new accelerators and new mechanics. By using the previous year's data or the current year's projected data, the analysis is actually an apples-to-apples comparison. The analysis may also alter the past performance for overall increased achievement and overall decreased achievement to test the sensitivity of the plan changes on total cost. For example, if the company achieves 5 percent more than last year, will more or less than 5 percent be spent on compensation, and what percent of revenue will be spent on incremental results? This work is done to finalize the formulas in order to ensure the variability is within an acceptable range.

Change in Individual Earnings. Here, the new plan designs and decisions are applied to the population on the plan to identify, at least conceptually, the "winners" and "losers" (in terms of earned incentive compensation) on the new plan. First, it is important to confirm that a change in the plan is meant to alter behaviors and results. Since the old plan did not reward that way, the new plan will pay differently, both for those that did well under the old plan with behaviors and results that are no longer acceptable, and for those who were doing the right thing but have not yet been rewarded for their results.

In this exercise, the population is rank-ordered by job type, from top change in positive earnings to top decrease in earnings. These rankings are reviewed for anomalies and then reviewed by the steering committee, which will inform the design team whether it is willing to live with these results or if the change is too dramatic. Once this decision is made, plans may be remodeled before being finalized. The final model will serve as a tool for management during implementation, because it will help explain the differences and the opportunities for shifts in sales activities and results.

Total Cost Compared to Budget. To complete this process, the incumbent model is used with any nonexisting salesforce members removed, any projected new salesforce members added and total-target cash earnings summarized. This amount must be compared to budget. If it is greater than budget, there is a basic planning problem, because TCC per individual has been increased beyond initial planning assumptions.

With an appropriate population (either projected or actual), the next step is to apply the historic and potential performance distributions with expected quotas/volumes for the coming fiscal year. *As a rule, approximately 60 percent – 65 percent of your salesforce must hit or overachieve its target performance levels for your company or sales team to hit its total number.* If that occurs, one-third will be earning less than target and approximately two-thirds will be overachieving and hitting accelerators. It is with this assumption that the comparison to budget must be made. *This typically means you will need to budget and may be spending somewhere between 105 percent and 110 percent of the summation of the total TCC for the team.* At this point, your company must address the fact that sales compensation spending and the budget must vary with achievement levels. Hence, the sensitivity analysis presented earlier must also be done so that payout volatility and totals can be built into budgets, forecasting and expense accruals in order to avoid financial surprises at fiscal year-end.

An illustrative costing scenario summary worksheet is provided as Figure 6-7. The worksheet provides the results of several achievement scenarios so that the cost of the new plan relative to revenue achievement can be appropriately assessed.

FIGURE 6-7 **Illustrative Costing Summary**

Background Numbers:

Prior-Year Goal	$1,200,000,000	
Prior-Year Actual Sales	$1,150,000,000	88% of goal
New-Plan Goal	$1,250,000,000	

Revenue Impact

New-Plan Scenarios	Annual Revenue	Revenue Change from Prior Year	Revenue as a % of New Goal	Revenue as a % of Prior-Year Goal
1 New-Plan Sales = Prior-Year Sales	$1,150,000,000	$ 0	92%	95.8%
2 New-Plan "Target"	$1,250,000,000	$100,000,000	100%	104.2%
3 New-Plan "Base"	$1,125,000,000	($ 25,000,000)	90%	93.8%
4 Between New-Plan "Base" and New-Plan "Target"	$1,187,500,000	$ 37,500,000	95%	99.0%
5 Above New-Plan Goal, but Below New-Plan Excellence	$1,312,500,000	$162,500,000	105%	109.4%
6 New-Plan "Excellence"	$1,375,000,000	$225,000,000	110%	114.6%
7 Above New-Plan "Excellence"	$1,437,500,000	$287,500,000	115%	119.8%

Compensation Costs Impact

New-Plan Scenarios	Prior-Year Total Compensation	New-Plan Total Compensation	$ Difference	% Difference
1 New-Plan Sales = Prior-Year Sales	$9,000,000	$ 7,611,675	($1,388,325)	-15.4%
2 New-Plan "Target"	$8,500,000	$ 9,472,703	$ 972,703	11.4%
3 New-Plan "Base"	$7,400,000	$ 7,500,000	$ 100,000	1.4%
4 Between New-Plan "Base" and New-Plan "Target"	$7,570,755	$ 8,200,000	$ 629,245	8.3%
5 Above New-Plan Goal, but Below New-Plan Excellence	$8,600,000	$11,200,000	$2,600,000	30.2%
6 New-Plan "Excellence"	$9,200,000	$11,800,000	$2,600,000	28.3%
7 Above New-Plan "Excellence"	$9,500,000	$12,600,000	$3,100,000	32.6%

Summing Up

Throughout the design process, you and the design team will be applying the data collected during your fact-finding, assessment and testing of your solutions with the management steering committee. The drivers come from multiple sources, and the degree of change must fit within the acceptable range of change for your company. Any resulting redesign decisions should go through the same process as the original design decisions. (Don't forget your objectives for the design – that is, what did you originally set out to do?)

The final cost assessment should be summarized for the steering committee, no small challenge, and filed with the design decisions. One of the most important things to remember is to make the process closed-looped. Come back at the end of the year, dig up the cost estimates and perform a detailed comparison of the results (often as part of the next year's assessment). Questions you should ask at that point include the following:

• What changed? Why?

• How much impact did it have?

• What can we do to make our assumptions stronger this year?

chapter 7
IMPLEMENTING A NEW PLAN

E ven the best-designed plans will fail if they are not implemented properly. Organizations with successful sales compensation plans devote the time and resources necessary to ensure that the new plan is fully tested and has gained support throughout the organization. They will educate the company, plan participants and management, and limit transition difficulties.

HR is frequently charged with developing the tools and programs related to implementing a new or revised sales compensation plan. Also, it may be asked by sales executives to assist with assessing the effectiveness of a new plan shortly after it is implemented.

This chapter describes processes, tools and concepts related to effective implementation of new or revised sales compensation plans:

• Common Transition Issues
• Developing the Implementation Plan
• Implementation-Process Roles
• Plan Modeling
• Implementation Tools
• Monitoring Change and Measuring Success.

Mastering the use of these implementation tools and processes will enable you to help your company increase the likelihood that the new sales compensation plan will achieve its desired objectives.

Common Transition Issues

No matter how small or how significant the change is in the sales compensation plan, there are five common transition issues that may become obstacles to success: (1) Resistance to new or changed sales role (see Chapter 6 for details on the drivers for this kind of change); (2) Lack of front-line sales managers' support for change;

(3) Objections to the new incentive strategy and plan mechanics; (4) Change in cash flow; and, (5) Failure of administrative systems. How these transition issues are addressed will have a major impact on the effectiveness of the new plan.

Resistance to a New Role

A new or revised sales compensation plan is frequently one result of a change in the sales job or implementation of a new role. As the HR professional working with the design team, you will want to be proactive in order to ensure that resistance is minimized when a new role is introduced. Frequently, that resistance may be the result of fear of the unknown ("What am I supposed to do in this new job?" or "How will this new job impact *my* career?"). Particularly with long-tenured employees, there is inherent disinterest in changing how they perform their jobs, especially if their approach to their jobs has been reinforced over time. Staffers, especially those that have been successful under the previous work and job models, often require a significant change-management effort to overcome that inertia.

To diffuse this potential challenge, you should work with sales management to provide affected employees with an advance orientation to the change. If the new role is one that will be staffed with current employees, there should be a well-defined development plan to help them gain the skills that are needed to succeed. You will also want to be sure there is sufficient time for learning to take place before the sales compensation plan used to reward success in the new role is implemented. Often an individually tailored vision of success under the new model and clear communication that the old model has been retired are the final pieces of the equation to create incentive for change.

Lack of Support from Managers

You probably have heard many times that the cornerstone to a successful plan is the support of the front-line managers. "If our managers don't like the plan, it will never succeed" is the basic belief in many companies. However, if front-line managers are not involved in the process of developing the plan and formulating the implementation process, it is quite likely that there will be field-management resistance. Two ways to help overcome that resistance are to involve selected front-line sales managers throughout the process, either as team members or team advisors, and to conduct "focus groups" on change with a broad group of managers. Both techniques provide meaningful opportunities for input. However, for either or both to succeed, the recommendations of the managers must be both acknowledged and used appropriately for whatever aspect of plan design or implementation their input has been solicited (including enforcement).

Objections to Measures or Mechanics

Possibly the single most common issue you will see is an objection to new measures or mechanics. Objections may be caused by concerns about the ability to succeed, the appropriateness of a new measure or the ease with which the members of the salesforce can estimate their earnings. However, beneath all these concerns is the perception that new measures or mechanics will have a negative impact on pay. This potential issue is unique, because it can occur even when the salesforce is willing to change. As part of the implementation process, you will need to work with finance and sales management to address these concerns. One very effective way to do this is by illustrating "old" vs. "new" plan payout for similar performance. These illustrations should be part of presentations, FAQs and management training that are designed to ensure that the intent and expected results of the new plan are made clear to the salesforce. As you build these communication tools, keep an informal tally of "concessions" to the salesforce and "take-aways" so that you know first whether salespeople are in a net negative or net positive situation under the new design. Use your knowledge of these factors to craft effective messages.

Change in Cash Flow

Even if the target payout remains the same or is greater than in the past, salesforce members' total cash compensation (W2 earnings) is based on both the actual payout of the incentive or variable portion of their compensation package and the timing of that payout. A change that seems simple, such as changing a component of the incentive plan from a monthly payout to a quarterly payout, may have a dramatic impact on the ability of plan participants to meet their basic financial obligations. Therefore, if the change will have an immediate and significant impact on cash flow for participants, a transition plan may be required before rollout. It may include financial planning assistance to help the salesforce member budget and pay recurring expenses, a transition guarantee for the first pay period or some other financial "safety net" based on performance. Helping the salesforce in this way is often an uphill battle, because skeptical or cynical salespeople may assume that any change is designed to benefit the company at their expense.

Failure of Administrative Systems

As discussed in Chapter 4, it is critically important to ensure that results can be measured, credited and reported accurately and on time before a measure is selected to be included in the sales compensation plan. Crediting rules must be in place and reflected in whatever system is used to measure and credit results, as well as link those results to the formula used to calculate payout. There are many steps from the sale to receiving payout for the sale (or other results required by the sales compensation plan), and each step in this critical process must be reviewed for accuracy and efficiency. While a plan may be well-designed, and the sales organization may be well-positioned for change, late or inaccurate payouts are significant obstacles to success.

Developing the Implementation Plan

Once potential challenges are recognized, and the degree of change has been assessed, a structured process should be used to guide the implementation of a new sales compensation plan. The process will address the following:

- Accountabilities: Who is responsible for each aspect of plan implementation – documenting the plan, creating payout examples, developing internal and field-training materials, scheduling rollout meetings?

- Specific changes: What has changed? What do the changes look like? How should they be explained? How can they be illustrated? What will the likely impact be on behaviors? On participant perceptions?

- How to determine whether desired benefits and improvements are being achieved: What are the expected behavioral changes? What financial and market results was the plan designed to support? How can the team best communicate these expectations? How can effectiveness be assessed and measured?

To develop an implementation plan that answers those questions and meets the needs of your organization, four factors need to be considered: adult learning, degree of change, timing and involvement of field managers.

- **Adult Learning.** When you are working on the implementation of a new or revised compensation plan, you should bear in mind that this is an opportunity for learning. Not only must plan participants understand the plan and what it means for them in terms of behavior and expected results, but managers also need to learn how to manage with the new plan. Understanding the following principles of adult learning will help you effectively influence the process of communicating and implementing a new sales compensation plan:

  – Motivation: Adults are goal-oriented and want to see the benefit of learning what is being taught. A sales compensation plan is relevant to the financial security and emotional sense of self-worth of the members of the salesforce. Their success under the plan has immediate relevance to their lives, and they are highly motivated to understand it. Thus, the method used to present, explain and illustrate the plan should be one that allows the salesforce to easily understand and internalize the plan.

- Reinforcement: Media and other tools should ensure that the message the company intends to convey by the plan is consistently and positively reinforced.

- Retention: Adults must see a purpose for what is being communicated so that what is learned is retained. The materials and media should include "practice" sessions to ensure that participants have direct experience in how the plan works and how they can affect the payout.

- Transference: The information that the media and materials convey must be transferred into positive action on the part of participants. The participants should be excited and want to use the information to enhance their opportunities.

Because there are many ways in which learning occurs, the full implementation plan should use materials and approaches that stimulate as many routes of knowledge acquisition as possible, such as visual stimulation through the use of slides and plan documentation, reinforcement through audible/spoken stimulation (presentation, Q&A, one-on-ones) and written reinforcement through practice sessions.

Degree of Change. If you are introducing a plan that is very different from past practices, all available resources should be used to ensure that it is understood and accepted. Typical reasons for plan failure all focus around lack of understanding of the need for change; that is, why new strategies are required or how new plan mechanics support those strategies. Ample time must be allocated to developing whatever materials and programs are needed. While practical considerations frequently take precedence over optimal implementation processes, you and the team chartered with implementation will need to confirm the financial, competency and headcount requirements associated with the implementation process. As a helpful tool in assessing those requirements, Figure 7-1 on page 118 summarizes the degree of change in the plan and the related timing and tools needed for successful introduction.

Timing. Several aspects will affect how much or how little detail should or can be addressed in the implementation process. If this is a midyear plan change, a full-scale implementation process is probably not practical or possible. However, key tools such as FAQs and plan documentation need to be revised to effectively address transition concerns and issues. If the design process has taken longer than anticipated and the new plan year has begun, large-scale training may be difficult to schedule and complete. However, the importance of a successful sales compensation plan is directly proportional to the focus and resources brought to bear on introducing and explaining it to all stakeholders.

Degree of Change	Changed Elements	Implementation Time*	Implementation Tools
Minor "Tweak"	Small change in mix or TCC Small change in quota or performance-measurement definition	30 – 45 days	Revised plan document Revised payout estimator
Moderate "Tactical"	Additional jobs eligible Significant change in mix New performance measure(s) Modified formula	45 – 90 days	All above New management and participant reports New performance measure(s) Leadership message Management presentation FAQs
Major "Strategic"	New organization New compensation structure New measurement methodology and structure New formula	90 – 120 days	All above New measurement and reporting system

FIGURE 7-1 **Degree of Change and Requirements**

* Implementation Time is the time required to ensure that systems are in place to support the plan, that the plan has been effectively introduced to the sales organization, that the plan is understood and that monitoring processes are in place.

Involvement of Field Managers. Despite the need for flexibility in functional and executive ownership of the sales compensation plan, it is imperative that front-line managers outwardly and explicitly embrace the plan as their own and that they do not describe it as "HR's plan" or "their plan" to their direct reports. The sales compensation plan is an important sales management tool, and there is no one better qualified than front-line management to provide information and direction about the communication/explanation detail that will be needed. Front-line managers can help you develop relevant and accurate questions and answers (FAQs); realistic scenarios that can be used to help members of the salesforce understand how the plan works; and other materials that will help them explain the plan.

Implementation-Process Roles

As described in Chapter 4, the design team includes members from several critical functions across the company. Even when the new plan has been approved, however, the team's job is not yet complete. To effectively implement and communicate the sales compensation plan, both headquarters and field resources are needed. Members of the design team will have a leadership role in communicating the plan's rationale and design.

The following plan communication and implementation roles are required, particularly if the plan changes are extensive or are likely to result in significant transition challenges:

- Sales Management: Senior sales management develops and delivers the change message – why change, why change now, how the new plan supports our strategy for the future. Field management ensures that direct reports understand the plan; confirm how it can use the plan as a management and recruiting tool; and then works with the implementation team to ensure that materials for rollout meet the needs of the field.

- Other Staff: HR ensures that the plan is consistent with corporate policies and competitive practice; works with legal and other resources on the development of plan documents and communication materials; participates in training sessions as needed; and works with other internal resources on ongoing monitoring and assessment. Sales administration is responsible for managing and administering the sales compensation plan and field measurement system, frequently in partnership with IT, finance and payroll. Systems/IT develops, assesses and maintains the tracking and measurement systems based on requirements defined by finance, sales management and sales administration. Finance works with sales administration and IT to ensure that measurement systems are in place, and leads the process of periodic assessment of plan effectiveness.

Plan Modeling

As described in Chapters 4 and 6, plan costing and modeling is an important task that the design team and other resources will complete as part of the design process. The results of the individual modeling are particularly useful as a tool in the implementation process, because the model can be used in training and individual sessions to illustrate the following important factors:

- How the plan works, that is, the formula and mechanics that are used to calculate payout

- The impact of various performance scenarios on payout

- Any differences between the former plan and the new plan.

As described earlier, this is particularly important when the new plan has changed significantly. Participant concerns about the impact of the change on their pay, their career and their future can be most realistically addressed by showing them exactly how the plan now works. In addition, the plan-modeling exercises are a useful tool when training field management in how the plan works and the results they should expect under it. There are several approaches to modeling, with inputs that range from simple to complex. The simplest models may use only headcount and target pay levels as inputs. More sophisticated models will include actual and hypothetical performance distributions, quotas, pay mix and period linearity assumptions or inputs in order to deliver more accurate and more sophisticated estimations of pay/expense so that finance can properly address the fully implemented plan in budgets.

In addition to addressing financial requirements, individual plan modeling is a process that will identify the potential impact on each individual year over year. To complete this level of individual-impact analysis, individual actual performance from the previous year is run through the proposed plan in the model, and payouts are compared to those of the previous year.

An aggregate of individual plan modeling can produce a displacement analysis that will help determine the total impact, positive or negative, on the salesforce. Displacement analysis sums the absolute value of each individual's change for the whole organization and divides it by the total sales compensation payout for the previous year. Displacement indices greater than 20 percent are viewed as significant changes with potentially catastrophic results, no matter how skilled your implementation team is. Even with a displacement index below 20 percent, sales management will typically want to see a list of the top 20 winners and top 20 losers under the new plan. It is important that these populations are accurate in terms of both role models and low performers.

Implementation Tools

As explained earlier, people learn in different ways. Especially in widely dispersed organizations, as many channels and media as possible should be considered in plan implementation. Figure 7-2 on pages 121 and 122 provides a summary of potential media.

While many templates may be in place for you to use, you and the design team should consider all the possibilities when developing or revising the tools that support an effective plan implementation. These tools include documentation and programs that clearly explain the plan and the business objectives it has been designed to support.

FIGURE 7-2 **Communication Media**

MEDIA SOURCE	EFFECTIVE USES	EXAMPLES	COST 1 Low	2 Medium	3 High	TURN-AROUND TIME TO COMPLETE
PRINT	• Conveys complex and detailed information • Reaches a wide audience • Can be used in conjunction with other media • Provides a written reference source • Excellent resource for training • Can generate program interest with a wide range of individuals	• Memorandum	X			1 week
		• Letters to employees	X			1-2 weeks
		• Handbook	X	X	X	6-8 weeks
		• Program-summary description	X	X		2-4 weeks
		• Brochures		X	X	6-8 weeks
		• Payroll stuffers	X	X		2-3 weeks
		• Informational flyers	X	X		1-2 weeks
VIDEO	• Excellent source for training • Conveys factual and emotional content • Provides a visual presentation to communicate program • Can be used to provide testimonials by senior leaders to support program • Can be used individually, or in large or small groups • Should be used in conjunction with printed media	• Major video production developed by an outside source	X	X		6-12 weeks
		• In-house production using leaders and employees	X	X		6-8 weeks
		• Small video clips offering testimonials or small bits of program information	X	X		4-6 weeks
AUDIO-VISUAL	• Provides consistent message • Should be used with other media • Provides a structured presentation • Can be used with small to large audiences • Conveys factual data and emotional content • Provides a visual application of the program • Provides opportunity for involvement by the recognition committee	• Narrated slide presentations		X		6-10 weeks
		• Speaker-led presentations with visual examples		X		
		• Program summaries tied to printed materials		X		6-12 weeks
AUDIO CASSETTE	• Provides literal translation to global and vision-impaired employees • Can reach a wide audience • Relatively inexpensive to produce • Can be used effectively with printed materials	• Audio cassette that provides complete program information	X	X		4-6 weeks
		• Short audio presentations to generate program interest	X			2-4 weeks

Continued on page 122

			COST			TURN-AROUND TIME TO COMPLETE
MEDIA SOURCE	EFFECTIVE USES	EXAMPLES	1 Low	2 Medium	3 High	
INTRANET/ INTERNET	• Can be excellent source for organizations with multiple locations • Provides factual information • Can be interactive and allows participants to comment about the recognition program • Geared to the modern employee who values technology • Reaches a wide audience • Can provide graphical representation	• Organizational Web sites		X	X	6-12 weeks
		• Intranet communication networks		X	X	Varies
		• E-mail	X	X		1-2 weeks if in place
GENERAL COMMUNI-CATION TOOLS	• Can be used to present the program to employees • Can be used in conjunction with other media • Can be customized to the audience or location • Facilitates discussion and interaction	• Slide presentations		X		4-6 weeks
		• CD-ROM		X	X	6-8 weeks
		• Overheads or other software presentation approaches (e.g. Power Point)	X	X		1-2 weeks

FIGURE 7-2 **Communication Media (Continued)**

Source: *Recognition at Work: Crafting a Value-Added Rewards Program* (WorldatWork, 2006)

Plan Documentation

Clear and accurate plan documentation must achieve the following objectives:

• Showing participants how the plan works; that is, shows them the details of performance measures and mechanics that are used to calculate payout

• Providing details about the various employment, measurement and legal policies and procedures associated with the plan.

Because of these two different objectives, plan documentation in many organizations may include two documents: (1) A short boilerplate plan description that includes the incentive opportunity, measures, goals and mechanics, and (2) A terms-and-conditions document that can be used for participants in many different plans. Because these are legal documents, the approval process must include review by legal. Figure 7-3 on page 123 provides a checklist of the factors that must be addressed in plan documentation regardless of the number of documents used in your company.

Once the formal plan documentation has been written (or revised, based on last year's plan), you should consider what other materials will be needed and who will be responsible for building those materials. For example, field sales management might work with you to develop a standard list of likely questions that will be

FIGURE 7-3 **Plan Documentation Checklist**		
Plan Mechanics	**Terms and Conditions**	**Employee Relations**
Plan effective dates	Account retention and movement	Benefit program impact
Performance measures	Audit procedures	Ethics violations
Performance standards	Bad debt, late receivables	Expense reimbursement program
Formula mechanics	Dispute resolution	Employment status: new hires, terminations, promotions, transfers
Quota determination and adjustments	Plan exceptions	
Thresholds, caps, other limitations	Sales crediting	Salary administration treatment/adjustments
	Territory definition	Time Off Impact

One final term is generally included in plan documentation: "The plan is not a guarantee of employment to any plan participant."

asked as the plan is rolled out. The design team members will provide the answers, and the FAQ will then be available for the training sessions, workshops and other implementation sessions as needed.

A plan calculator is another tool that can help the salesforce understand the plan quickly. How often have you heard that members of the salesforce have created their own worksheets, complete with complicated formulas, to estimate what their payout will be under the new plan, given various performance scenarios? Thus, a very attractive implementation tool to offer the sales organization is a plan calculator or payout estimator. This tool is usually in a spreadsheet application and allows salesforce members and sales managers to create their own performance and payout scenarios. Providing this kind of tool to the salesforce typically results in a significant savings of time that translates into more time available for selling.

Training for Managers and Internal Resources
Often overlooked in plan implementation is the development of training sessions for internal staff and field-based managers. Training provides a learning environment for those responsible for all aspects of administration and those who will use the plan. Why is this so critical? Managers need to be equipped to explain the plan and to use it effectively as a management tool. Internal resources that will be responsible for plan administration need to understand the details of the plan, including the performance measures, level of measurement, crediting rules and formula used to calculate payout. Consistency of the message is important here; presentation materials and the notes used by the trainers must support the message the plan has been designed to deliver.

Internal training should be done well in advance of actual plan introduction so that all associated resources are equipped to execute their roles in plan communication and administration. Internal training is a task that is assigned to functional-area experts on the design team. These team members have the most detailed information about the plan, and they know the requirements for tracking, measuring and reporting performance. The same people may also be charged with actually conducting training sessions for employees who are responsible for day-to-day activities related to plan administration.

In order to develop materials and provide training to internal resources who support plan success, your organization must do a good job of training sales managers in how to manage the salesforce under the new plan. Sales management members of the design team and steering committee should be asked about the approach and amount of detail needed for this training. However, a training session for front-line managers generally covers the following topics:

- How to use sales compensation as a sales management tool
- The organization's business objectives and sales strategies for the plan year
- Rationale for changing the old plan
- The new plan – objectives, key features, plan-calculation formula and how it works (with practice examples)
- Performance objectives or goals and how they are assigned
- How to answer likely questions, including puts and takes for various roles relative to the old plan.

Venue Choices for Plan Introduction

Based on the extent of change in the sales compensation plan, potential transition issues and the time available, there are several alternative approaches to plan introduction. However, no matter how small or significant the alteration, broad and focused communication of the leadership message about change is critical to success – what is different, why and how it may impact plan participants.

That message and the related training/learning and discussion should be delivered in the venue that is most appropriate for the degree of change, as follows:

- For major plan changes, everyone should hear the same message at the same time – for example, at the national sales meeting or at a series of world region meetings. A high-visibility rollout should include a general session in which the senior sales leader delivers the leadership message about change. Breakout sessions for further discussion in smaller groups can also be held. This large-scale introduction should always be preceded by front-line and staff training on the new plan so that questions asked in breakout sessions can be answered immediately and accurately. Plan participants should leave the large-scale session with a good understanding of the new plan, why it is important and how they can succeed under it.

- For widely dispersed sales organizations, or in those cases where the plan changes are essentially tactical and easily explained, using alternative media (Webcast or online training) can be effective. Because the opportunity for dialogue is limited in this approach, a very tightly scripted slide presentation accompanied by very clearly articulated talking points is required. Helpful materials to provide to the participants include the plan documentation, FAQs and several illustrative scenarios.

Whether the introduction is at a national meeting or at local sales meetings, personalized management discussions with the salesforce after a more formal presentation will help ensure that the message is clear, the plan details are understood and each individual knows what he or she must do to succeed.

Monitoring Change and Measuring Success

After a new sales compensation plan is implemented, management is interested in knowing about its effectiveness in contributing to desired results so that any design problems can be caught early and fixed. Thus, a well-defined process for monitoring the results of change and assessing whether the intended results are being achieved is an important element of the implementation plan. Examining business success under a new sales compensation plan is, in fact, a subset of analysis and evaluation that is typically associated with plan assessment. Thus, an HR professional has the opportunity to once again apply the knowledge and skills described in Chapter 5 to assist sales executives with post-implementation assessment.

Measuring the success of a new sales compensation plan typically involves looking at the following two areas:

- Financial Results: Most companies are interested in improving the sales return on dollars spent on sales incentive compensation. In the past several years, many companies have successfully shifted from thinking about sales compensation as an expense to thinking about it as an investment. For this reason, both sales executives and financial executives are interested in knowing about financial performance under the new plan. Typical questions include: Is the compensation cost under the plan appropriate for the level of expected sales results? In general, are sales employees more productive? That is, is the average sales per salesperson improving compared to the previous year? Are the top producers doing as well under the new plan as they did in past years? Is the company growing its business as expected? Is the company achieving its revenue and profit goals?

- Employee Acceptance: Essentially, sales executives are interested in knowing about the plan's effectiveness in retaining talent and redirecting and/or reshaping salesforce selling behavior and performance. The most typical questions they are likely to ask are: Is the plan viewed as competitive and equitable? Do the field sales managers feel it is effectively supporting and rewarding desired behaviors and results? Is it motivating the salesforce to alter its sales behavior in the desired manner? Were members of the salesforce enthusiastic about the new plan when it was announced, and were they still enthusiastic after the first payment under the plan? These questions are the ones that the HR professional should anticipate sales executives will ask. However, if these questions are not posed, a company should think seriously about asking them after the new plan is in place.

As part of the implementation process, there should be a defined approach and set time frame established for measuring success under the new plan. Measurement should be performed both initially and on a regular basis throughout the year. The HR professional should encourage and work with sales executives to map out how the company will measure success under the new sales compensation plan based on the objectives the plan was designed to support. Failure to measure success may mean that important inconsistencies or drawbacks in the new plan are not recognized and addressed in time to make a difference in sales behavior and business results during the plan year.

The HR professional can help the company focus on the following aspects of measuring success:

- Facilitating the assessment of plan effectiveness in achieving desired objectives
- Surveying sales employees' attitudes about the new plan.

Facilitating the Assessment of Plan Effectiveness in Achieving Desired Objectives

When assessing the impact of a new sales compensation plan, it is important to understand plan objectives; that is, to answer the question: Why was the plan changed? Ideally, the answer to that question will be contained in the new plan description and the presentation materials used to launch the plan. The objectives for the plan and expectations for results have already been agreed to as part of the design process and confirmed when the plan was finalized.

Increasingly, companies are changing their sales compensation plans to focus salesforce attention on one or more or the following objectives: revenue growth, customer retention and expansion, new product sales, sales profitability (for example, either gross margin or product mix) and cost/productivity improvement. The specific objectives of a particular plan will determine both the effectiveness metrics and the types of analyses that should be performed. However, at a high level, the goals of assessing effectiveness within 30 to 90 days of launch are as follows:

- Determine whether management's expectations for the new plan are or are not being achieved.
- Measure to what extent or degree the expectations are or have been realized.
- Identify potential problems areas in the plan that may have come to light after the first payment under the plan.

One area of plan assessment that is attracting a great deal of attention is sales compensation ROI. In fact, a WorldatWork survey reports that 86 percent of participants indicated that how to determine ROI is the most important challenge faced by their company.[1] Top management is interested in the extent to which sales compensation dollars, particularly variable pay, are being paid for the same business sold last year or incrementally new business sales. Therefore, compensation cost of sales (CCOS) analysis is important. In particular, variable pay expense – commission, bonus or both – should be compared to gains in the following:

- Revenue (or revenue vs. plan)
- Margin – dollars, percent or both
- Other business plan goals; for example, customer mix, product mix
- Personal (salesforce member) productivity
- Retention of top performers (that is, lower than competitive turnover).

Key diagnostic tests, year-over-year, should be performed to determine if sales compensation dollars are being spent wisely. Those tests should include the following analyses:

- Percent achievement of (sales) financial goals – revenue and margin
- Pay dispersion
- Differentiation between top and marginal performers
- Pay: financial performance correlation; and pay: appraisal scores correlation
- Year-over-year compensation variability, particularly for top performers
- Quota performance distribution vs. desired or projected distribution.

---

[1] Jerome A. Colletti and Stockton Colt, "Identifying a Complex Sales Environment: Results of a Special Member Survey," workspan, April 2004.

The HR professional can provide guidance to the plan-assessment process by ensuring that metrics are tailored to the plan's specific objectives and that data required for analysis is available for measurement in future periods on an ongoing basis.

Surveying Salesforce and Manager Attitudes About the New Plan

After the plan has been introduced to the sales organization, it is helpful to confirm that the message received was the message intended and that participants understand the details and requirements. The best time to assess this is after the first payout under the plan. An effective way to assess perceptions and determine the degree to which the plan is impacting behavior is to conduct a relatively short survey. Whether the survey is conducted via the Web, by e-mail or by some other method commonly used in your company, its effectiveness will be greater if the respondents are assured of a reasonable degree of anonymity.

Sales management and the design team can use survey results to assess the following:

- The degree to which participants understand the new plan
- The organization units and employees that may need additional training
- Elements of the plan that are perceived positively and those that may become problems
- Implementation issues that have been overlooked.

Conducting the survey year over year can help you and others on the design team assess the degree to which plan changes are understood and working as intended. The sample questionnaire provided in Chapter 3 can easily be tailored to your specific plan details and changes.

First-line sales managers should also be included in such survey efforts. In addition to asking them the same questions asked of the salesforce, two other sets of questions should be considered. First, it would be helpful to know if front-line managers believe members of the salesforce have changed their behavior as a result of the new plan, and if so, whether they believe that the change is consistent with desired results. Second, it would be helpful to know if front-line managers believe that they would have benefited from additional information or help in launching the new plan. Knowing if managers feel additional help would have been beneficial is useful when planning for implementation training in subsequent years. Figure 7-4 on page 129 is a sample of the additional questions that could be asked of front-line sales managers.

Questions	Check One Response		
	Yes	No	Unsure
The salesforce's behavior has changed as a result of the new sales compensation plan.			
If you checked "Yes" to the previous question, has the change been positive?			
Please briefly explain your response.			

Areas Where You Would Like Additional Help or Information
(Rate each statement, where 5 is the highest importance and 1 is the lowest, by placing an "X" in the appropriate box)

Statement	5	4	3	2	1
The labor market(s) information our company uses to set incentive pay rates					
Base salary ranges and incentive targets for each field sales job					
How performance weights (individual vs. team) are determined; and why they are what they are					
The fundamentals of managing with incentive pay, e.g., how to talk with the salesforce about the plan, how to answer questions					
Communications, e.g., what to say/what not to say					
How to explain why various performance measures were selected for the plans					
Performance planning, e.g., how to set objectives					
Career-planning and incentive opportunities, i.e., how to talk about what the salesforce can look forward to in higher-level position(s)					
Other (write in) _____					

Additional Comments
Please share with us any additional comments that you have about the incentive plan(s) that you believe will be helpful to us.

Midcourse Reviews and Corrections

While changing a plan during the year may cause some disruption and consternation among participants, it is important for the design team to focus on results at the end of each payout or performance period. Rather than allowing issues and problems to accumulate throughout the year, periodic reviews provide the opportunity to correct critical errors. Finance and sales management should design analytics and reports that provide senior management with the information needed to assess results in a timely manner based on the objectives the plan was designed to support. An example of a first-period and ongoing-assessment checklist is presented in Figure 7-5.

		FIGURE 7-5 **Initial Assessment Checklist**
Yes	**No**	**Question for Analysis (Financial, Survey, Performance) to Answer**
		Do the members of the salesforce fully understand the structure of their compensation plan and their expected performance on the plan?
		Is the organization performing as expected on the compensation plan?
		Is payout correlated to performance? (Are par performers earning target or above, "best" performers earning upside as anticipated and marginal performers earning significantly less than target?)
		Are all components of the plan operating as expected?
		Are total pay levels and incentive pay levels positively correlated with business (revenue, volume, profit, market share) performance?
		Do all members of the salesforce fully understand their performance expectations? Do they understand how these expectations relate to their compensation plan and to the company's total goals?
		Is the company performing as expected with regard to attaining its sales goals?
		Does goal attainment significantly differentiate top performers from average and marginal performers? Is performance distributed as expected across the organization?
		Has the company provided accurate monthly performance data on each measure to corporate? To each participant?
		Has the company performed as expected on market, customer and financial metrics?

Companies generally do not expect to make midyear changes to the sales compensation plan. A recent survey reports that 70 percent of the respondents indicated that their sales leaders/executives were not contemplating a midyear change to the compensation plan.[2] However, from time to time, changes to the business or erratic economies cause companies to consider midyear change

---

[2] Jerome A. Colletti and Mary S. Fiss, "Keeping Your Sales Reps in the Game: Survey Results and Interpretation, CF Websurvey, Fall 2004.

because they are concerned about the loss of talented people, important customers or both. In many businesses, first-half results are often a clear indictor of whether a company and its salesforce are on track with meeting plan goals.

Consider this case: Only 25 percent of XYZ company's salesforce was at or above the year-to-date revenue plan compared to 60 percent who were at or above the year-to-date plan in the same period in the previous year. This result was during a period of an erratic economy, and thus management was concerned about what action to take. Ultimately, management decided to lower the performance threshold to enable more members of the salesforce to gain entry into the incentive plan. However, how they reached that conclusion is as important as the decision itself. Their thought process included the following points:

- Don't overreact. Changing the sales compensation plan prematurely sets a bad precedent.

- Revalidate growth goals; for example, where growth will come from and whether the size of the goal is realistic relative to market opportunity.

- Examine the history of business results. Q3 and Q4 in many industries represent a significant proportion of the business. It is wise to examine how business is trending as Q2 draws to a close. If it appears that business is rebounding, even slowly, a change in the compensation plan may not be required.

- Examine payout history. For example, what percent of the salesforce was "in the game" in the same period during the previous year?

- Examine productivity, particularly of top performers. What is the percent of top performers this year compared to the previous year?

The HR professional can serve as the voice of reason in situations where midyear plan change is being considered. Because most companies are committed to not compromising their sales pay for performance culture, management needs assurance that midyear plan change is the right action to take. For that reason, the HR professional should play an informed and active role in midyear plan-change discussions.

Summing Up

No sales compensation plan is complete until the company implements it and evaluates the results it helps to achieve. Was the plan launched effectively? And is it doing what the company wants it to do? The only way to authoritatively know the answers to these two important questions is to ensure that a carefully thought-out implementation plan is developed and used to launch and evaluate the new plan.

Understanding why a plan was changed and what results are desired from it is a key consideration when evaluating its success. It is important to know whether members of the salesforce are being motivated and rewarded to achieve the results desired under the new plan. And in situations where the expected outcomes are not being achieved, it is important that the company acts quickly to take corrective action. As explained throughout this chapter, the HR professional can make important contributions to the success of a new sales compensation plan by playing an active role in developing implementation tools and materials and by suggesting approaches to measure the plan's success.

chapter 8

ALIGNING OTHER REWARDS AND RECOGNITION PROGRAMS

Sales compensation is a critical link in the business-management chain. However, it is not the only link. Well-defined performance objectives, positive feedback based on a formal assessment process, and formal and informal recognition programs can be used by sales leaders to create and foster a positive and productive salesforce culture. While the sales compensation plan may provide the most immediately visible feedback on performance, companies frequently find that the plan alone cannot do the whole job of rewarding and recognizing contributions. Thus, there are other programs that are used to direct, motivate and reward the salesforce.

HR usually is the function responsible for both base pay and other corporate rewards programs. You are therefore likely to be involved in contributing to the design of other programs for the salesforce, as well as assessing the impact of such programs on the salesforce and advising management on the recommended ways to use them. In the following sections, this chapter describes those programs and also provides suggestions about how they can be integrated with and complement the sales compensation plan:

• Tie to Total Rewards

• Pay Increases

• Formal and Informal Add-On Programs

• What Can Possibly Go Wrong?

Tie to Total Rewards
As described in Chapter 2, sales compensation is likely to be only one element of the total rewards offered to the salesforce by your company. The total compensation package for the salesforce may include one or all of the elements that are available for nonsalesforce employees in a company.

With few exceptions, members of the salesforce are eligible for direct and indirect financial rewards, including benefits, some type of base pay and incentive/variable pay (also known as *sales compensation*). Base pay and benefits are typically designed to provide a level of financial security to the salesforce; however, these may be provided at a somewhat discounted rate because the salesforce is eligible for sales incentive compensation. Formal or informal *add-on* programs may also be components of the total rewards system for these jobs. Such programs are typically designed to recognize and reward skills, achievement, tenure or a variety of other factors that contribute to the company's success. While base pay, variable pay and benefits are critical elements in the total rewards picture for the salesforce, other programs may be important to provide support for affiliation needs/recognition and to provide positive reinforcement related to work content.

The other incentive programs described in this chapter are used as complements to the sales compensation plan. They include formal programs such as base pay increases, short-term contests (quarterly), long-term recognition programs (annually) and informal practices. The HR professional should be familiar with these and should be prepared to help sales executives properly align them to the sales compensation plan.

Pay Increases

The "100-percent commission" sales job still exists in some industries, including insurance and stock brokerage, as well as transaction-selling businesses that are conducted door to door, over the telephone and in retail-mall kiosks. However, the cash compensation package for most sales jobs includes an element of fixed pay – either wage or salary – depending on the type of sales job and its FLSA status. Historically, many sales jobs have been paid a uniform salary (that is, the same fixed pay was available for each sales job in a company, so no salary range or band was used for those jobs.) This *fixed pay* approach has become less dominant, and sales jobs generally are paid based on the wage or salary structure available for jobs at similar levels and with the same exemption status within the company.

Salary is a fixed payment made with defined frequency; it may be adjusted to reflect the cost of labor, skills, seniority and performance. A wage is the money rate, expressed in dollars and cents, paid to an employee per hour. Whichever type of payment is used, base pay provides some financial security to the salesforce, and a base pay increase can be the most predominant additional program available to motivate and reward performance of a salesforce, particularly if it is adjusted based on specific drivers.

Base salary is earned through the satisfactory performance of the primary duties of a job and any additional (secondary) activities required by a company's management and/or customers. Each person's base salary is typically structured to compensate for the level of skill, experience and dedication brought to the job. Several drivers are associated with a change in base pay: company initiatives, changes in the job, new market realities, incumbent performance or tenure. Whatever the driver, base pay delivers a message to the salesforce that should complement the message associated with the sales compensation program: "This is the performance and these are the behaviors we need from you in this job."

As the HR professional working with sales, you may be charged with the responsibility of ensuring that pay levels are competitive and that the range of pay is appropriate for the job. As described in Chapters 4 and 5, you will need to confirm the charter of the job and the factors used to price the job to the market. Once the salary or wage program is defined for the sales jobs in your organizations, the process and tools used to determine any pay adjustment must also be aligned with the requirements of the jobs.

In nonmerit-oriented cultures, base pay may only reflect the tenure of individuals and cost-of-living adjustments (COLA). However, in merit pay plans, a merit increase in base salary is generally based on a formal performance-review process that factors in the primary aspects of the job. This program frequently includes performance measures outside the incentive plan such as "how" the results are achieved. Through appropriate factors or objectives, the program should accurately reflect the differences between sales jobs and other jobs at the same level in the organization. If you are responsible for performance-management programs at your company, you will need to confirm that the process, definitions and program details reflect the expectations for the sales job, and truly reflect the right performance standards.

Formal and Informal Add-On Programs

As described in Chapter 2, the elements of total cash compensation for the salesforce are base pay and an incentive compensation opportunity. Based on company and market practice, a benefits plan may also be available. These components will meet the financial security needs of the salesforce. There are, however, *work experience* needs such as affiliation and work content, as described in the *Rewards of Work* study[1] that can be best supported by other formal or informal recognition practices and programs. Two such types of programs commonly used with a sales organization are contests and recognition programs. Figure 8-1 on page 138 provides a summary of the differences between these two types of programs.

---

[1] Paul W. Mulvey, Gerald E. Ledford, Jr. and Peter V. LeBlanc. (Third Quarter, 2000.) "Rewards of Work: How They Drive Performance, Retention and Satisfaction." *WorldatWork Journal*.

	Informal Recognition	Contest	Formal Recognition Program
FIGURE 8-1 Contests and Recognition Programs			
Other Names (AKA)	Pat on back (also known as, "Atta boys/girls!") Spot awards	SPIFF	Rewards and Recognition
Time Frame	Immediate	Shorter term (1-6 months)	Longer term (annual or multiple years/consistency)
Objective	Provide immediate positive reinforcement of contribution through acknowledgement and praise	Reward specific achievement of short-term objectives	Reward-balanced performance over a longer period of time to drive consistency and support culture

Contests

Sales contests are used to stimulate the achievement of short-term sales objectives. Contests and special performance incentives for field force (SPIFFs) typically are developed with sales and marketing and may focus on a particular product, market or type of customer. Sales contests are an effective tool for focusing salesforce efforts and can be useful in recognizing specific achievements that are not rewarded through the sales compensation plan. Examples of contest objectives are provided in Figure 8-2.

FIGURE 8-2 Illustrative Contest Objectives and Parameters

Contest Measures for This Year
- Q1: Stimulate sales of Product A and Product X
- Q2: Increase market penetration in defined urban geographies
- Q3: Introduce Product Line CD extensions
- Q4: Convert competitive accounts

Eligibility
- Inside and field salesforce, customer-service reps
- Sales and customer service front-line managers

Award
- Cash awards, based on level of achievement
- "Everyone can win"

Although cash is the most typical reward for contests, payment may also be in the form of prizes, plaques or public commendation. Unlike earnings under the sales compensation plan, this compensation should always be considered add-on rather than at-risk compensation. It is generally funded from outside the sales department. For this reason, SPIFFs or contests are typically not included in salary benchmark data by the large survey houses. However, some survey houses have started to collect this information in order to report on practices, policy or total cash compensation components.

As described in Chapter 3, overuse of SPIFFs or contests is a potential problem. While they are considered an effective motivator, as the HR professional you will want to ensure the following:

SPIFFs are not being used as a sales management safety net when the sales compensation plan does not appear to be paying top performers appropriately (for example, when sales quotas are considered unreachable but contests can deliver incentive payout regardless of quota achievement).

Overuse of contests is not diluting focus on the key measures in the incentive plan (for example, when product marketing introduces several SPIFFs for new products or products under competitive threat, even though the products are not critical to achievement of the business plan).

Members of the salesforce are not frequently forced to choose between where they should spend their time – contest or sales compensation plan measures (for example, acquiring new customers or selling new products vs. retaining and growing current accounts).

A correct balance is struck in targeting the right number of "winners" (achievable but exclusive) and the significance of the reward (attractive but not distracting) in order to support behavioral motivation best practices.

The contest measures are aligned with the philosophy, ethics and business focus of the organization.

Sales contests and SPIFFs have proven to be tools that are used too frequently or for inappropriate reasons (such as delivering pay in a down year) by some companies. Organizations should therefore strive to keep the total payout for SPIFFs at or below 10 percent of the total sales compensation budget.

Rewards and Recognition Programs

Recognition programs or rewards and recognition (R&R) programs are widely used in many industries. Many types exist; the most common ones used by customer-facing organizations are listed in Figure 8-3 on page 140. Within the sales organization, you are likely to see highly regarded R&R programs such as the trip or quota club, which are designed specifically to reward the highest sales achievers and thus those that have significant sales compensation earnings. However, there are other reasons to design and implement a recognition program that acknowledges and recognizes the contributions of many members of the salesforce. Recognition and praise, whether informally given or as part of a formal program, offer many positive benefits, including increased engagement, higher satisfaction and greater loyalty. They also frequently increase productivity in the long run. These programs are critical elements in the total rewards picture because they meet specific needs beyond financial security and are useful in motivating, rewarding and retaining valued employees.

FIGURE 8-3 **Types and Examples of Recognition**[2]

	Type and Description	Examples
Formal: A structured program designed to reward and recognize individuals for high levels of achievement according to specific criteria.	**Financial Awards:** Programs that provide either a fixed cash award or are based on a percent of the employee's pay. Some cash awards programs can provide additional employee benefits that have a stipulated dollar value. These may be short-term contests or longer-term recognition programs.	Lump-sum bonus Additional cash incentive, e.g., contests Additional paid time off Stock options Paid trip, e.g., quota trip Stock award program Gift certificate Specialized training
	Symbolic Awards: Recognition programs designed to provide a tangible award or memento that is valued by the recipient.	Plaques and trophies, e.g., president's club, Tenure or service awards, e.g., 10-year club Achievement awards, e.g., rep of the year, 1005 club

	Type and Description	Examples
Informal: An expectation of managers/supervisors to give praise in public or private, with or without a tangible award.	**Verbal Recognition:** Provides praise directly to the individual or team	Management thanks in public or private Thank-you card Testimonial from senior leadership Customer feedback Public recognition
	Spot Award: Low or minimal cost, no formal document or extensive administration; provides immediate recognition	Paid meal Tickets Gift card

[2] *Recognition at Work: Crafting a Value-Added Rewards Program* (WorldatWork, 2006)

R&R programs are generally chartered at the corporate level and may be developed and administered at that level or at lower organizational and/or geographic levels. Members of the salesforce may therefore participate in R&R programs that are companywide, specifically designed for customer-facing jobs or developed and administered for their team, specialty or geography. Whichever the case, recognition programs, like the sales compensation plan, must provide a reward that is based on performance. However, these programs focus on long-term objectives and continuity. They may use objective or subjective performance measurements, or both.

Unlike the sales compensation program, there are several types of rewards that can be offered: cash, prizes, intangibles (such as time off), plaques and other visible awards. You may be asked to weigh in on the most appropriate type of award for these programs. In order to provide awards that are valued by the recipient, fact-finding should be completed to determine what would be most valued by eligible participants. A rule of thumb is that the award should be both valued and visible. That is, there should be some ability to receive acknowledgement from others for having received it by having the award made publicly, or by being externally visible in some other manner.

While management may believe that cash is the most valued reward and the easiest to implement, rewards need not be financial to be valued. Providing even more cash incentives has several disadvantages: it dilutes the message of the sales compensation program and limits the "external message" value of the award because it is not visible to others. Other tangible awards, such as trips or merchandise, provide high visibility without diluting the sales compensation plan objectives. An alternative is PTO (paid time off), which may be considered as "extra pay," but retains the advantages of other tangible awards – visibility (without divulging the monetary value) and the ability to share the award with loved ones.

Nontangible awards can include participation in a valued meeting or seminar, or public acknowledgement of the person's contribution. For example, verbal and public recognition of an individual's contribution by someone "two levels up" (for example, the second-level manager recognizes a sales representative) is generally considered highly motivational. In fact, in many studies, employees cite non-monetary recognition as having a longer-lasting impact than monetary rewards.

Budgeting and forecasting should be reasonably accurate, or management might endanger the motivational power of the recognition program by retroactively trimming the eligible population to stay within budget. Companies planning the budgets for intangible recognition programs like trips tend to use 1 percent to 2 percent of the total sales compensation budget as a guideline. This would represent approximately 20 percent of the salesforce achieving the recognition level and a prize value of 5 percent – 10 percent of target sales compensation for the achieving population.

Informal Recognition

Informal recognition can take the form of a spot award or a simple personal and verbal statement of appreciation. While spot-award programs are less commonly used in sales organizations, there are several advantages to using this type of less-formal recognition: the cost is generally low, the benefits of immediate positive reinforcement are high and the possible negative consequence of monetary or career envy is low. While this type of program should have guidelines and a budget, it is typically not considered a formal recognition program and can be used very successfully by managers of customer-facing employees to reinforce desired behaviors or outcomes.

Possibly the most important factor for retaining key members of the salesforce is the relationship with the front-line manager. Thus, in your organization, one of the most critical practices you can reinforce is the value of informal, immediate praise and recognition. Your front-line managers should be expected to acknowledge and recognize the contribution of the salesforce in all aspects of the job – not simply volume or quota achievement. This is truly *informal recognition* and may be the most effective tool your managers possess for acknowledging their employees' value and contributions.

To be successful, you will need to ensure that the contributions rewarded by a thank-you card or a spot award are consistent with company philosophy, job requirements, and the standards set forth in your performance appraisal system. While extensive training may not be required for managers, a consistent set of guidelines and periodic assessments will help ensure that your salesforce is being recognized for contributions that cannot be rewarded through the sales compensation plan.

What Can Possibly Go Wrong?

Additional reward programs such as merit pay increases, contests and recognition programs can be very positive reinforcers and motivators. However, unless feedback is clear and objectives are well-defined and do not compete from program to program, problems can develop. Symptoms to watch for include the following:

- Disregard for company policies ("win at all costs")
- Friction between management and the salesforce ("I want to win this award, not focus on your objectives")
- Motivational let-down ("I expected a good raise")
- Confusion ("what is it they want us to do?")
- Lack of team cooperation ("if you win, I lose").

Summing Up

Pay increases and reward programs are useful management tools for recognizing and rewarding skills, behaviors and achievements not rewarded through sales compensation, or for reinforcing the behaviors required to succeed. To be successful, programs must support your company's culture and philosophy, and align with the business strategy. (For example, rewarding for tenure may be at odds with the "pay for performance" objectives of sales compensation.) It is critical to ensure that contests and other reward programs do not deliver a conflicting message to the salesforce about desired behaviors and results.

chapter 9

GOVERNANCE OF SALES COMPENSATION PROGRAMS

"The fox is guarding the henhouse." This cliché captures some of the concerns of both HR and finance regarding the effectiveness of sales compensation plans. Sales is often the only organization that fully understands how corporate strategy will be translated into sales strategy, selling processes, sales roles and ultimately the sales compensation plan. If other functions or resources come into the picture after these decisions have been made and attempt to influence compensation design and administration with insight and authority, they will be buried within the compensation plan. Crediting issues, gaming opportunities, pay inflation and extra expense can be interwoven so tightly in the final sales compensation plan that it is almost impossible to address and resolve them after the fact. On top of this, shareholders and Congress impact the process through Sarbanes-Oxley. Now, the CEO and CFO can go to prison if errors that are deemed unethical occur in the sales compensation plans and it is found that there was knowledge of these errors or "inadequate controls." That fact alone has driven management to exert increased control and *governance* over sales compensation. While terms and conditions (T&Cs) have always been a fundamental element of a well-designed sales compensation plan, they focus primarily on explaining various administrative and employment aspects and are often not enough by themselves to support governance. Governance implies that a system for authoritative control is in place related to the program. While some sales executives may perceive governance as excessive control, in fact a good governance model can be applied to sales compensation without robbing the organization of its flexibility to respond to labor markets, customer needs and competitive opportunities. In some cases, it may even benefit sales employees, as T&Cs are beefed up to include formally documented dispute and exception processes.

With that in mind, this chapter has two objectives presented in the following sections:

- Compensation Governance
- Communication and Process Gaps

- Common Sales Compensation-Related Governance Problems
- Demystifying Sarbanes-Oxley
- A Detailed Governance Model
- Leadership
- Central vs. Local Control
- Meetings, Voting, Notes, Documentation.

First, this chapter describes the challenges associated with effective sales compensation governance. Second, it explains how you can address and resolve those challenges at your company. Examples and techniques are provided that have been successfully used by leading companies.

Compensation Governance
Governance associated with compensation programs begins at the highest level of control. *Board governance* is essentially the checks, balances and due diligence necessary to ensure that C-level (CEO, COO, CFO, CXO, etc.) executives do not make short-sighted decisions that benefit themselves at the expense of shareholder value. Because of the complex legal, accounting and reporting issues that must be considered, the compensation committee of the board of directors typically handles executive compensation packages for top executives.

Sales compensation plans are short-term and cash-based (as opposed to long-term and equity-based) and do not typically come before the board compensation committee for approval. It is generally believed that the CEO, COO, CFO, head of HR and head of sales have enough counterbalances among them to come to a win-win solution. However, because this is not always the case, there are several aspects of sales compensation plans that require sound governance principles. As discussed in earlier chapters, sales compensation design and administration is a complex cross-functional exercise. If any one participant becomes too strong in the process, or if ideological gaps exist between participants, governance becomes even more important to sales compensation.

Communication and Process Gaps
There are four basic gaps that a sound governance model helps to overcome. Because these are the places where corporate strategy and policies can lose their meaning and power if companies are not careful, you should be familiar with these gaps and how to close them at your company. They include the following:

1. The gap between senior management and front-line managers
2. The gap between functions (such as HR, sales and finance)

3. The gap between business units (BUs) with distinct profit-&-loss (P&L) responsibility

4. The gap between geographies that may or may not have different laws and subsidiaries (legal entities).

Gap Between Senior Management and Front-line Managers

The gap between senior management and front-line managers typically is a problem of communication and alignment.

Communication. If senior managers do not take pains to communicate strategies and tactical plans to the field, it can be expected that there will be deviation, malicious or not. It takes many repetitions of simple concepts to build a unified vision. Therefore, an investment of time is necessary. However, field communications is an area in which there is significant underinvestment by senior management.

Alignment. Alignment of plans is important to ensure that top management's equity and profit-based plans do not compete entirely with middle management's cash and revenue-based plans and the front line's revenue and activity-based plans. This is a check that is often best performed after distinct role-based sales compensation plans have been designed. It is also something to be wary of if sales management's compensation plans are designed in a separate effort from the front-line plans. Both communication and alignment are areas where you can have considerable impact as the sales compensation plan is being designed and during rollout and ongoing follow-up. Poor communication and alignment put governance in a deficit position from the start.

Gap Between Functions

The gap between functions is generally one of communication and expectations; this is one of the most difficult tactical issues to control during the sales compensation design process. Different functional goals may result in competing agendas, and intelligent compromise may be difficult to achieve. Clearly defined functional roles and accountabilities are critical to closing any difference in expectations. The concept of segregation of responsibilities is important to good governance. If the aforementioned functions are the last accountable reviews for various distinct metrics and conditions, the organization can feel somewhat more comfortable that irregularities have been ironed out and a consensus solution for the common good has been achieved.

Gap Between Business Units

The gap between business units (BUs) is a more delicate matter. The use of business-unit P&L responsibility to empower leaders yet hold them accountable for results is a powerful management tool. However, these BU leaders may not have a good view of the complete picture of success for the corporation as a whole. On top of that, their management skills may not be as strong as those of the corporate leadership team. They may lean heavily on a few management tools (such as the sales compensation plan) or capitalize on approaches or models that do not make the most sense for the company as a whole or for the long term. These leaders are often internal customers of shared corporate services that must work with them to deploy sales compensation plans. Strong operating principles and design frameworks that provide reasonable local flexibility with some centralized control are necessary to bridge this gap. The same governance principles must apply to the growth segments as well as the mature lines of business, regardless of how much more challenging their performance goals might be.

Gap Between Geographies

The gap between geographical regions within a multinational corporation is still a sensitive issue despite years of moving toward globalization. The business practices accepted in some countries may appear flawed at best when taken out of context and printed on the front page of the *Wall Street Journal*. HR professionals have long recognized the difficulty of deploying consistent sales compensation plans across geographical and political boundaries. Whether it is the tax treatment of bonuses in Canada or the advance notice of intended changes required by the Works Councils in Europe or the less aggressive pay mixes dictated by some Asian cultures, it has always been challenging to manage across these complex organizations.

True, sales resources in these countries are becoming more receptive to traditional North American pay-for-performance structures. But in spite of U.S-based businesses' recent focus on business ethics and governance, some remote regions do not always feel a sense of urgency to get on board. Corporate governance processes should be in place that can be used with appropriate adjustments across geographies, as those regions are ready to implement a formal control system.

Common Sales Compensation-Related Governance Problems

Problems related specifically to the sales compensation plan are positioned on top of these systemic issues that require an authoritative system of control. Sales organizations have historically maintained their own control over the sales compensation program, contrary to the new focus on the importance of a sound governance process and distinct accountabilities. As the HR professional in your organization who works with sales, you should be able to talk with sales executives about the benefits of improved processes and clear roles. The best approach to building support for governance within sales management may be to focus on the frustrations that sales already has with sales compensation (see the assessment results from Chapter 5). The most common issues associated with a lack of governance in the sales compensation program are as follows:

- A "let's make a deal" approach to sales compensation plan design that results in multiple plans for one job or different measures for the same job

- Missed targets, either sales or expense or both, because: (1) quotas are adjusted downward without regard for the total business target that needs to be achieved, or (2) upward adjustments are made to sales credit, the payout formula or the final payout based on a plan exception or management discretion

- Unintended negative behavioral consequences

- Frequent calculation errors and either disgruntled members of the salesforce (if payout is late or there is an underpayment) or financial issues because of overpayments.

With the recent focus on enhanced governance infrastructure, one does not have to dig very deep to uncover criminal and civil cases based on lapses of sales compensation governance. The interesting thing about most of these cases is that while finance is often focused on the expense of the sales compensation plans, the most serious infractions involve dysfunctional behaviors and illegal activities to drive the revenue side of the equation. If the plan's CCOS (compensation cost of sales) is over 5 percent of revenue, it is definitely "material," but cost overruns can be written off to "unforeseeable circumstances" and only impact two to three stakeholders (salesforce, senior management, shareholders), while improperly booked revenue involves a more premeditated act and draws in the fourth stakeholder, the customer.

The following are recent examples of such dysfunctional behaviors and illegal activities:

- Both the CEO and the head of sales of a large software company pleaded guilty in 2004 to federal securities fraud. They were guilty of, among other things, extending the last month of fiscal quarters (to 35 days in some cases) to allow additional sales to be booked, thereby exceeding analyst estimates and fraudulently driving up the stock price and the value of their options.

- Several executives, including members of the salesforce, at a large wholesale telecommunications company were convicted of criminal charges in 2004 because they exchanged dark fiber (unused fiber-optic cable) between two companies, essentially yielding no net flow of goods or services in either direction, and yet booked the transactions as sales with associated revenue. The sales compensation plans in place had extremely aggressive pay mixes.

- Another telecommunications company was named in civil litigation based on "cramming," the act of adding services to a consumer's bill that were not ordered. The Communication Workers of America (CWA) backed the telesales resources involved (against management) based on the belief that the sales compensation plans encouraged this activity.
- A manufacturing company experienced dramatically increased sales compensation costs, and ultimately stock price volatility, after senior executives decided to "invest" in several customers in exchange for excessively large orders of product. The customers went public and made money on their investments, then went bankrupt because their business models were flawed. The members of the salesforce assigned to those accounts received large commission payouts, but the customers failed to pay their invoices.
- A sales representative at a consumer packaged-goods company confided that whenever he needed to move extra product to hit his goal, he had cooperative retailers who would accept extra inventory stashed in their stockrooms.
- A publishing company that oriented its sales compensation plans to drive for new accounts found that several salesforce members were canceling existing accounts so that they could sign them back up as "new" and receive increased payouts under the sales compensation plan. Customers neither saw nor felt any change in their status, but profitability at the company was negatively impacted.

The common factor for most of these situations is that sound compensation administration and detailed reporting would have probably uncovered them sooner and allowed management to mitigate the damage. The shorthand for these processes and reports is the "adequate controls" described in Sarbanes-Oxley.

Demystifying Sarbanes-Oxley

In 2002, Congress passed the Sarbanes-Oxley Act as a response to scandals at Enron, Tyco and other public companies. The act is intended to "protect investors by improving the accuracy and reliability of corporate disclosures." In reality, House Resolution 3763 is 66 pages of well-meaning but vague legalese. (See Figure 9-1 on page 151 for a list of its contents.) Many of the Act's 11 "titles" (chapters) address issues such as auditor independence and increased penalties for corporate fraud. These have very little impact on the HR professional's involvement in sales compensation design and administration. The sections that do have implications are fairly isolated and short:

- Section 302, Corporate Responsibility for Financial Reports: This section states that the CEO and CFO must certify each annual or quarterly report. It then goes on to state what they are certifying – "... that ... the report does not contain any untrue statement of a material fact or omit to state a material fact necessary to make the statements ... not misleading ... ," that "... the signing officers are responsible for establishing and maintaining internal controls ... designed ... to ensure that material information ... is made known to such officers... ," and that there will be an "... audit ... [to identify] all significant deficiencies in the design or operation of internal controls ... ." Essentially, this is stating that there is no plausible deniability when it comes to the kinds of mistakes described above in a public company's financial statements.

- Section 401, Disclosures in Periodic Reports: This section states that a company must disclose off-balance sheet transactions that have a "... material current or future effect on financial condition ... ." This could be construed as impacting several types of sales transactions that include related binding promises or financing.

- Section 404, Management Assessment of Internal Controls: This section is very similar to Section 302, but adds the responsibility for "adequate" internal controls and management's responsibility for assessing and reporting on the controls' adequacy.

FIGURE 9-1 **Contents of Sarbanes-Oxley Act**

Title I –	Public Company Accounting Oversight Board (establishes this body with its composition, funding and authority)
Title II –	Auditor Independence (Sets rules for selection and rotation of independent auditors for public companies)
Title III –	Corporate Responsibility (outlines the responsibilities of the audit committee, insider-trading issues and penalties)
Title IV –	Enhanced Financial Disclosures (Sets a code of ethics for top executives and establishes new reporting requirements to demonstrate internal controls)
Title V –	Analyst Conflict of Interest (Establishes new rules for securities analysts and the relationships they can have with publicly traded companies)
Title VI –	Commission Resources and Authority (Further outlines authority and practices of the commission)
Title VII –	Studies and Reports (reviews impacts of accounting-firm consolidation and investment-bank restructuring)
Title VIII –	Corporate and Criminal Fraud Accountability (Establishes criminal penalties for altering documents, protection for whistle-blowers and sentencing guidelines)
Title IX –	White-Collar Crime Penalty Enhancements (Increases penalties for mail and wire fraud, violation of ERISA)
Title X –	Corporate Tax Returns (Establishes that all corporate tax returns must be signed by CEO)
Title XI –	Corporate Fraud and Accountability (Addresses additional rules and guidelines for document tampering and other offenses by corporate officers or board members, increases penalties established under the Securities Exchange Act of 1934)

A Detailed Governance Model

A more detailed outline of "adequate controls" is necessary, primarily because, as with most government legislation, it isn't spelled out for the concerned executive anywhere else. Three basic concepts should be addressed for governance to be adequately addressed:

- Accountability: It must be clear which functions and people within the organization are accountable for which results and adherence to which policies. This accountability should be reinforced by the organizational structure, performance metrics, performance evaluation and compensation plans themselves. It should ensure that the intended results are built into each person's job description and that only people who follow the rules and deliver the intended results receive positive evaluations and target (or higher) bonuses. The organizational structure issue is more a function of removing obstacles and improving "lines of sight" than of developing any groundbreaking design.

- Alignment: The strategies and goals of the organization must be clear and must deliver value to shareholders. The processes and systems required to support them must align with those objectives. Where necessary, explicit decision-support tools should supplement the processes. Overall, implementation of this alignment creates a cultural expectation that all activity must drive real, substantial shareholder value (not just short-term increases that allow top executives to exercise their options). This culture should be intolerant of fraud and supportive of whistle-blowers.

- Accuracy: Data to support financial reporting and sales compensation crediting must be accurate from all regions and channels. There should be a paper trail to support auditing of that data. Rules and regulations should be accurately communicated and enforcement and penalties accurately applied. Performance evaluation must be based on an accurate picture of that performance and payout formulas accurately applied and calculated.

As complex as this may sound, it is merely a representation of sound business practices when displayed in its basic state (see Figure 9-2 on page 153). Documentation of these activities and programs is the element that is often missing. Companies tend to view documentation as important to the degree that they have had issues with enforcement. Companies without a history of legal problems or with strong cultures of accountability may keep basic electronic and paper files of meeting minutes, votes on key decisions and reported metrics. However, companies negatively impacted in the latest round of investigations have committed to go the extra mile and document every step of every process.

Excluding enforcement of generally accepted accounting principles (GAAP), many of these activities or concepts are within HR's scope of expertise. You should work with finance or the internal audit team to assess each area, looking for conflicts of interest, weak systems or undocumented processes, and to make recommendations for improvement. The deadline for responding to Sarbanes-Oxley has come and gone, and many companies are still struggling to demonstrate "adequate controls."

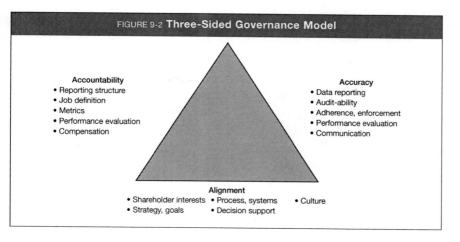

FIGURE 9-2 **Three-Sided Governance Model**

Accountability
- Reporting structure
- Job definition
- Metrics
- Performance evaluation
- Compensation

Accuracy
- Data reporting
- Audit-ability
- Adherence, enforcement
- Performance evaluation
- Communication

Alignment
- Shareholder interests
- Strategy, goals
- Process, systems
- Decision support
- Culture

Leadership

Ultimately, the accountability comes back to executive leadership. Companies that are best prepared to deal with sales compensation governance issues are those that have top executives that will stand up, accept ownership and champion the program. HR has as much potential to lead this effort as any function. (Note: A powerful ally for HR in this effort may be legal if it is willing and able to exert an opinion on sales compensation governance.) The ideal executive champion should do the following:

- Have some experience with the motivational power and potential complexity of sales compensation.

- Be able to influence and marshal resources from other departments.

- Represent decisions made by the sales compensation team and outline the supporting arguments for those decisions to outsiders.

- Have the authority to restructure the composition of the sales compensation team as deemed necessary to execute on the company's strategy and governance model.

Keep in mind that one trade-off with a strong leader in sales compensation is the increased importance of checks and balances for approvals. If your organization is still struggling with the deployment of effective governance processes and practices, look first to the leadership of the effort for serious commitment and the other characteristics described here.

Central vs. Local Control

A strong, central, corporate leader of sales compensation, while a tremendous asset, will also sometimes lead to questions about centralized versus local control in sales compensation. The presence or absence of regional leaders who share a strong sense of accountability, alignment and value of accuracy will further complicate these questions. The most successful companies typically have structured a framework that explicitly retains certain decision rights for central corporate resources while empowering local resources to make other specific decisions to suit their unique business environment and strategies. These decision rights should be documented in both the governance framework and the sales compensation T & Cs. A logical division of these might be as follows:

- Centralized: Market-benchmark percentile, role eligibility (there must be an objective standard as to the skills and experience necessary to be assigned to a role, and participants should not be able to make that judgment themselves), performance measures, some formula mechanics, quota-setting process, most crediting rules (typically matching the quota-setting principles regarding duplicate or split credit), key policies concerning employment status (for example, transfer, leave of absence), pay administration.

- Localized: Pay level, pay mix, upside, weightings of performance measures, some formula mechanics, pay frequency, individual quotas, supplemental policies.

Additional responsibilities can be moved in either direction as manpower and culture warrant. As more activities and decision rights are moved toward the local geographies or BUs, the central corporate lead will want to consider the need for "satellite" design teams to parallel the design work and process taking place at headquarters. This assumes that there are local/regional resources in finance, marketing and HR that are up to the task. Likewise, as responsibility moves outward to local regions or BUs, most companies will increase investment in the audit side of the equation. Empowerment is smart, and scrutiny is smarter. An inability to implement tailored tactics is a symptom of a sales compensation program that is too centralized. Plan proliferation, increased cost and loss of control are symptoms of a program that is too decentralized.

Meetings, Voting, Notes, Documentation

As your organization works through the carefully structured and documented process you created based on the information in Chapter 4, you will have several scheduled or ad hoc meetings to confirm plan issues from the assessment, plan-change objectives, expense budgets, system capabilities and testing requirements, communication strategies, midperiod plan (or quota or territory) changes and emergent-issue resolutions. To conform with good governance principles, you should make sure that these meetings are attended by the full team (sometimes a tremendous challenge in schedule management – you may need to literally cancel meetings that are partially attended). Key decisions that require a vote of the team members should be explicitly stated as requiring a single authority to approve, a majority to approve, a super-majority (67 percent) or full consensus. The results of any votes should be documented in meeting minutes, and the minutes should be filed (electronic and paper copies) for future reference and auditability. Meetings of regional design teams, corporate-governance councils and/or steering committees should have established distribution lists for decisions and documentation so that information is flowing in the right directions to provide consistent governance.

Summing Up

Governance is a concept that sounds complicated but is really a reinforcement of sound management principles. If you have followed the advice in the previous chapters regarding the establishment of explicit, documented compensation philosophies, design and administration processes with assigned roles and responsibilities, and cross-functional design teams and steering committees, you are already more than halfway toward a sound sales compensation program with a foundation of good governance. To complete the model, decision rights and results must be documented and you must be diligent in your analysis of plan performance and process reinforcement. Disputes and issues in both design and administration must be escalated to the correct authorities, who must act without conflict of interest. The biggest obstacles in the quest for improved sales compensation governance may be your corporate culture or the inertia of some executives. Sarbanes-Oxley, while not creating radically new thought in terms of governance structure, may well be the impetus for change with its increased accountability and penalties for top management.

SELECTED REFERENCES

Articles
(www.worldatwork.org/library)

Albrecht, Chad. 2001. It's Not All Relative: Pitting Quotas Against Other Incentive Plans to Motivate Sales Performance. *WorldatWork Journal*, Third Quarter, 59-64.

Anderson, Jeremy; Petrucci, Antoinette. 2002. New Reality in High Tech Sales Pay. *workspan*, March.

Blackburn, Jan; Bremen, John M. 2003. From Exporting to Integrating Optimizing Total Rewards for a Global Sales Force. *WorldatWork Journal*, 4th Quarter.

Bremen, John M.; Blackburn, Jan; 2003. Where is Sales Compensation Heading in 2003? *workspan*, January, 46-52.

Brown, Brad. 2002. Rewarding Results: The Road to Sales Compensation Excellence. *workspan*, January.

Choos, Raoul; Surdel, Robert. 2005. Mastering the Solution Sales Reward Puzzle. *workspan*, December, 27-31.

Cichelli, David. 2004. Does Sales Compensation Need More Corporate Oversight? *workspan*, June.

Colletti, Jerry; Colt, Stockton. 2004. Identifying a 'Complex' Sales Environment: Results of a Special Member Survey. *workspan*, April.

Colletti, Jerry; Fiss Mary. 2005. *Are You Using the Right Measures of Performance in Your Sales Compensation Plan?*

Colletti, Jerry; Fiss Mary. 2005. *Are You Ready for Sales Compensation Plan Tweaking?*

Colletti, Jerry; Fiss, Mary. 2005. *Diets for the SIP Plan Document.*

Colletti, Jerry; Fiss Mary. 2005. *Expecting Too Much From "Relationship Selling" Can Lead To Poor Incentive Design.*

Colletti, Jerry; Fiss Mary. 2005. *Factors Determining the Salary/Incentive Ratio.*

Colletti, Jerry; Fiss Mary. 2005. *Gambling on Sales Compensation to Fix a Business.*

Colletti, Jerry; Fiss, Mary. 2005. *Getting The Right Results Through the Sales Compensation Plan.*

Colletti, Jerry; Fiss, Mary. 2005. *A Global Perspective on Regional Pay Differentials.*

Colletti, Jerry; Fiss, Mary. 2005. *Incentive Strategies for Keeping Sales People in the Game.*

Colletti, Jerry; Fiss, Mary. 2005. *Integrated Sales Performance Management: Practical Suggestions to a Perennial Problem.*

Colletti, Jerry; Fiss, Mary. 2005. *Involving Business Leaders in the Sales Compensation Design.*

Colletti, Jerry; Fiss, Mary. 2005. *Keeping Your Sales Reps in the Game: Should an Erratic Economy Impact the Incentive Plan?*

Colletti, Jerry; Fiss, Mary. 2005. *Making Sense Out of Sales Performance Management Programs.*

Colletti, Jerry; Fiss, Mary. 2005. *Managing with Sales Incentives: Are Your Front Line Managers Well Prepared to Manage with Next Year's Plan?*

Colletti, Jerry; Fiss, Mary. 2005. *Measuring Sales Compensation ROI:Part 1, How to Think About It.*

Colletti, Jerry; Fiss, Mary. 2005. *Measuring Sales Compensation ROI:Part 2, What Metrics to Use.*

Colletti, Jerry; Fiss, Mary. 2005. *Perspectives on Compensating Complex Sales.*

Colletti, Jerry; Fiss, Mary. 2005. *Perspectives on HR Involvement with Sales Compensation.*

Colletti, Jerry; Fiss, Mary. 2005. *Planning Sales Growth After a Successful Year.*

Colletti, Jerry; Fiss, Mary. 2005. *Rethinking Sales Compensation Plans to Support Top Line Growth.*

Colletti, Jerry; Fiss, Mary. 2005. *Retooling for Sales Growth.*

Colletti, Jerry; Fiss, Mary. 2005. *The Role of Base Salary in Sales Compensation.*

Colletti, Jerry; Fiss, Mary. 2005. *Rx For Successful Sales Performance Management.*

Colletti, Jerry; Fiss, Mary. 2005. *Seven Symptoms of a Failing Sales Compensation Plan.*

Colletti, Jerry; Fiss, Mary. 2005. *Some Important Thinking About Why Sales Compensation Works.*

Colletti, Jerry; Fiss, Mary. 2005. *SPIFF: Unraveling Its Meaning and Use.*

Colletti, Jerry; Fiss, Mary. 2005. *Techniques to Use for Expressing The Sales Incentive Pay Opportunity.*

Colletti, Jerry; Fiss, Mary. 2005. *Thoughts About How Leaders Increase Sales Effectiveness.*

Colletti, Jerry; Fiss, Mary. 2005. *Thoughts About Sales Leadership in Times of Top Line Growth.*

Colletti, Jerry; Fiss, Mary. 2005. *Thoughts About Total Rewards and Sales Compensation.*

Colletti, Jerry; Fiss, Mary. 2005. *Using Sales Credits "Uplifts" As An Incentive Alternative.*

Dallas, Michael. 2001. Metamorphosis of Winning Sales Compensation. *workspan*, August.

Donnolo, Mark. 2005. Check your Sales Compensation Report Card. *workspan*, January, 56-61.

Feder, Ira. Fine-tuning the Pay Mix for Potential Cost Savings. *WorldatWork Journal*, Second Quarter, 6-7.

Gauthier, Bill. 2002. The Sales Compensation Challenge: Meeting the Diverse Needs of Multiple Business Units. *workspan*, March.

Knight, Thomas G. 2005. Sales Compensation Plans for a Recovering Economy. *workspan*, January, 63-66.

Mercer, William M. 2000. *Improving Sales Performance.* 1-8.

Mercer, William M. 2003. *Managing Your Sales Force Investment In Any Economy.*

Mercer, William M. 2003. *Optimizing the Sales Effort To Jump-Start Growth.*

Pekkarinen, Michael; Ulrich, Craig. 2003. Do We Have It Right? Sales Optimization Indicators Help Manage Sales Force Investments in Any Economy. *WorldatWork Journal*, 3rd Quarter.

Pentolino, John. 2002. Making the Case for Sales Incentive Administration Software. *workspan*, January, 8-10.

Reiman, Paul J. 2004. Are Your Sales Compensation Plans Working as Designed? *WorldatWork Journal*, 4th Quarter, 16-24.

Riley, Lisa J. 2001. Little Things Make A Big Difference Selling A Sales Compensation Plan. *workspan*, May.

Serino, Bonnie. 2002. Noncash Awards Boost Sales Compensation Plans. *workspan*, August.

Ulrich, Craig D. 2005. Heal the Achilles Heel of Sales Management. *workspan*, November, 36-39.

Weeks, Bill. 2002. Running on Empty? Managing Sales Compensation Costs in a Slow Market. *workspan*, January.

WorldatWork Live Chat Transcripts

(www.worldatwork.org /Networking/Live Chats/Transcripts)

Catch the Wave of Economic Recovery with Sales Compensation (Canadian Chat) Guest speaker: David Johnston.

HR's Role in Sales Compensation Design. Guest Speaker: David Cichelli. Part 1 and Part 2.

Sales Compensation: Are You Getting What You're Paying For? Guest Speaker: Stockton Colt.

WorldatWork Surveys

(www.worldatwork.org Go to Library/Research/Surveys and select surveys from the menu on the right)

2005. Key Sales Incentive Plan Practices.

WorldatWork Bookstore

WorldatWork. 2002. *The Best of Sales Compensation: A Collection of Articles from WorldatWork*. Scottsdale: WorldatWork.

Cichelli, David J. 2003. *Compensating the Sales Force*. New York: McGraw-Hill.

Colletti, Jerome A.; Cichelli, David J. 2005. *Designing Sales Compensation Plans*. Scottsdale: WorldatWork.

Colt, Stockton B. Jr. (Editor). 1998. *The Sales Compensation Handbook*. New York: AMACOM.

WorldatWork Courses

C5: Elements of Sales Compensation

Sales Compensation Design: Developing Next Year's Plan

Sales Compensation for Complex Selling Models

Outside Resources

Cocks, David J. and Dennis Gould. (March 2001). "Sales Compensation: A New Technology-enabled Strategy." *Compensation & Benefits Review*. 33(1):27-31.

Conlin, Bob. 2005. Sales Compensation as a Strategic Business Tool. *MX Magazine*, March/April.

Dorf, Paul R. (Summer 2000). "Designing Compensation to Boost Sales Performance." *National Productivity Review*. 19(3):73-77.

Rauch, Maggie. 2005. Getting Rewards Right. *Incentive Magazine*, July.

Reiman, Paul J. 2005. A Structured Approach to Sales Compensation Integration. *Sibson Perspectives*, Volume 13, Issue 1.

Stiffler, Mark A. 2005. Pay for Performance. *Pharmaceutical Executive*, July.

Sands, S. Scott. (April 2000). "Ineffective Quotas: The Hidden Threat to Sales Compensation Plans." *Compensation & Benefits Review*. 32(2):35-42.

Zimmerman, Eilene. (January 2001). "Quota busters." *Sales & Marketing Management*. 153(1):58-62.

Zingheim, Patricia and Jay Schuster. (December 2000.) "Performance pays." *Pharmaceutical Executive*. 20(12):68-72.

GLOSSARY

Term	Definition
agent/broker	Member of an indirect sales channel who sells products but does not take ownership of goods.
award	An amount of cash, a prize, a symbol or an intangible reward given as a form of recognition. Awards can be in the form of money, prizes, plaques, travel and public commendations. The payouts of sales contests usually are called "awards."
base pay	The fixed compensation paid to an employee for performing specific job responsibilities. It is typically paid as a salary, hourly or piece rate.
benefits	Programs that an employer uses to supplement the cash compensation an employee receives. Benefits include income protection programs such as publicly mandated and voluntary private "income protection" programs that often are provided through insurance, pay for time not worked and other employee perquisites.
BlueBird	See windfall.
bonus	An after-the-fact reward or payment (may be either discretionary or nondiscretionary) based on the performance of an individual, a group of workers operating as a unit, a division or business unit, or an entire workforce. Payments may be made in cash, shares, share options or other items of value. In the context of sales compensation, a defined, pre-established amount of money to be earned for achieving a specified performance goal. Planned bonus amounts commonly are expressed as a percent of the incumbent's base salary, salary range midpoint, percentage of target cash compensation or

incentive compensation, or a defined dollar amount. See also discretionary and nondiscretionary bonus.

cap
The total incentive opportunity that can be earned in a given period. Cap may also refer to the maximum cash compensation an employee may earn in a given time period.

combination pay plan
A combination pay plan has two elements: a base salary and one or more cash incentive components, such as a bonus or a commission.

commission
A payment based on a formula that is used to calculate the incentive compensation opportunity for salespeople. In this context, it provides a predetermined incentive amount for each discrete unit of sales made by the salesperson. Commissions commonly are expressed as a percent of each sales dollar (revenue), percent of gross margin (profit), or a dollar amount per unit sold. A commission-only compensation program is sometimes known as "full commission" or "straight commission."

compensation
Cash provided by an employer to an employee for services rendered. Compensation comprises the elements of pay (e.g., base pay, variable pay, stock, etc.) that an employer offers an employee in return for his or her services.

cost of labor
A measure of external pay practices where data on labor market costs (total compensation amounts) are obtained from labor market competitors and relied upon when establishing target cash compensation opportunity. It reflects a "cost to hire and retain" logic for setting target pay levels.

cost of sales
For sales compensation purposes, a relative measure of internal costs. It reflects an "ability to pay" logic for setting target pay levels. The cost of sales, expressed as a percent, is calculated by dividing the total sales dollar volume sold by the sales force into the total or aggregate cash compensation costs of the sales force.

cumulative performance period
For sales incentive calculation purposes, a type of performance period in which an incumbent's performance is accumulated and measured over time, and compared against goals that are

also accumulated over various performance periods. For example, while incentive payouts might be made each month, actual performance for a salesperson might be accumulated in each successive month of a quarter and compared against accumulated goals. As an illustration, in the second month, the incumbent's performance is the sum of the performances of the first two months compared with the sum of the performance goals for the same two months.

direct channel   Manufacturers and service providers in a direct channel, service the end customers directly; they do not use external distribution channels.

direct seller   In sales compensation, one whose objective is to obtain an order from the end user.

discrete performance period
Relative to employee performance, a type of performance period in which the performance of the incumbent is limited to a defined performance period without any connection to past or future performance periods. As an example: "Each month is discrete, because performance is measured for that month and payout is made for that month independent of past or future performance in other months."

distributor/wholesaler
Selling member of an indirect channel who buys and resells another company's products.

draw   A compensation payment that is paid in advance of performance. There are two types of draws: recoverable and nonrecoverable. In both cases, if performance produces incentive earnings in excess of the draw, then the sales representative receives the additional monies beyond the draw amount. If the sales representative's incentive earnings are less than a recoverable draw, then the sales representative must return the amount of the draw that was not earned, or the unearned amount is carried forward to the next performance period. However, with a nonrecoverable draw, if the incentive earnings do not exceed the draw, draw monies are not returned or carried forward – the sales representative gets to keep the draw.

eligibility for a plan
The basis for determining the individuals or classes of employees eligible to participate in a particular plan such as an incentive or a supplemental benefits plan. This eligibility may be based on salary, job grade, organization unit or function or a number of other criteria.

flat commission   Commission rate does not vary.

gross margin   A profit measure: sale price minus the cost of goods before overhead, profits and taxes. Gross margin may be used as a performance measure in sales compensation plans.

guarantee   For sales compensation purposes, a compensation payment, possibly in addition to base salary, that is made regardless of performance. It is usually nonrecoverable. Guarantees may be temporary or permanent.

incentive   Any form of variable payment tied to performance. The payment may be a monetary award, such as cash or equity, or a nonmonetary award, such as merchandise or travel. Incentives are contrasted with bonuses in that performance goals for incentives are predetermined.

indirect channel   Manufacturers and service providers in an indirect channel use one or more levels of distribution (e.g., distributors, wholesalers, retail stores and agents) to reach customers.

internal equity   A fairness criterion that directs an employer to establish wage rates that correspond to each job's relative value to the organization.

job scope   Magnitude of accountability for the job.

leverage   As used for sales compensation purposes, leverage is the amount of increased or "upside" incentive opportunity – in addition to target incentive pay – that management expects outstanding performers to earn.

market pricing   Relative to compensation, the technique of creating a job worth hierarchy based on the "going rate" for benchmark jobs in the labor market(s) relevant to the organization. Under this method, job content is considered secondarily to ensure internal equity after a preliminary hierarchy is established based on market pay levels for benchmark jobs. All other jobs are "slotted" into the hierarchy based on whole job comparison.

maximum   Relative to sales compensation, the total incentive opportunity a sales representative can earn in a given time period. The term may also refer to the total cash compensation an employee may earn in a given time period. Sometimes a maximum is referred to as a "cap," "ceiling" or "lid."

mean   A simple arithmetic average obtained by adding a set of numbers and then dividing the sum by the number of items in the set.

median   The middle item in a set of ranked data points containing an odd number of items. When an even number of items are ranked, the average of the two middle items is the median.

mix   Relative to compensation, the relationship between the base salary and the planned (or target) incentive amounts in the total cash compensation package at planned or expected performance. The two portions of the mix, expressed as percentages, always add to 100 percent.

nonmonetary awards
Noncash compensation, such as travel and merchandise. It excludes other nontaxable items (not on W-2 form) such as gifts and plaques/pins.

pay at risk   A variable pay plan funded on the basis of a reduction in base pay that usually is offset by the possibility of a larger variable pay plan payout.

pay survey   Gathering, summarizing and analyzing data on wages and salaries paid by other employers for selected key classes of jobs or benchmark jobs.

payout frequency
The timing of incentive payouts. Payouts commonly are made weekly, monthly, quarterly or annually.

performance period
A predetermined span of time during which individual (or group) performance is measured.

progressive incentive formula
A rewards program in which the incentive payout rate increases as performance exceeds predetermined levels (e.g., nonlinear sales commission formulas).

quota	A predetermined performance goal. Quotas can be expressed as absolute numbers, a percent (100 percent), percent change or units sold. Also referred to as goal, objective and performance target.
quota setting	The process of setting quotas. Quotas can be established by senior management ("top down"), by the field sales force ("bottom up") or through a negotiated process involving both headquarters and the field sales force ("combination").

ramped commission

Commission rate changes after an objective has been met. The rate may either increase (progressive) or decrease (regressive).

range of earnings The amount of total cash compensation opportunity available for minimum to excellence performance.

recognition program

A policy of acknowledging employee contributions after the fact, possibly without predetermined goals or performance levels that the employee is expected to achieve. Examples include giving employees clocks or other gifts on milestone anniversaries, granting an extra personal day for perfect attendance or paying a one-time cash bonus for making a cost-saving suggestion.

regressive incentive

In a regressive incentive formula, the incentive rate declines as performance exceeds pre-established levels.

revenue The money generated by a company from sale of goods or services including rental income. Often referred to as sales in manufacturing and merchandising companies.

sales channel The means a manufacturer or service-providing company might employ to interact with and manage relationships among its final, end-user customers. Such channels might be direct, in which the manufacturer uses a sales force to sell to its end-use customers, or they might be indirect, such that the manufacturer employs a third-party company to represent its products to the marketplace of customers.

sales compensation

Monetary amounts paid to sales representatives or sales management that vary in accordance with accomplishment of sales goals. Sales compensation formulas usually attempt to establish direct incentives for sales.

sales contest   An event entailing a short-term sales effort to maximize results for a nonrecurring purpose in an effort to win a prize. Usually short in duration, such contests are designed to be supplemental to the regular sales compensation program, not to replace it.

sales cycle   The time, starting with identifying the customer (prospect), it normally takes to close the sale.

sales event   An occurrence when a sale may be counted for compensation purposes.

shortfalls   A sales result significantly below expectations which is not influenced by the sales representative.

split credit   The division and assignment of sales credit to more than one salesperson.

target cash compensation (TCC)

As it relates to sales compensation, the total cash compensation (including base salary and incentive compensation) available for achieving expected results.

target performance

The expected and/or planned level of sales results. It is often called the "quota" or "goal."

the work experience

See work experience.

threshold   The minimum level of performance that must be achieved before an incentive can be earned.

total rewards   The monetary and non-monetary return provided to employees in exchange for their time, talents, efforts and results. It involves the deliberate integration of five key elements that effectively attract, motivate and retain the talent required to achieve desired business results.

upside potential   See leverage.

variable commission

Commission rates in a particular incentive plan are not constant and may vary depending on the salesperson's performance or on the particular measurement used.

windfall　A sales result that was realized outside the normal influencing role of the sales representative. Because the sales person had low or no involvement in creating the sale, a windfall is sometimes excluded from normal incentive compensation treatment.

work experience　Elements of rewards that are important to employees but may be less tangible than compensation or benefits. It includes acknowledgement or recognition of effort/performance, balance of work-life issues, cultural issues, development opportunities and environmental factors.

ABOUT THE AUTHORS

About the Authors

Jerome A. Colletti is managing partner of Colletti-Fiss, LLC, a management-consulting firm headquartered in Scottsdale, AZ. His firm is a leading source of expertise and insight on strategic compensation issues affecting the productivity of sales and customer contact employees.

A management consultant since 1977, Jerry provides advice to top managers on the design and implementation of compensation plans, particularly variable pay arrangements, to reward employees for sales success, customer retention and customer loyalty.

He is the author of more than 70 publications and has been a Cert 5 (Elements of Sales Compensation) course instructor for WorldatWork since 1979. In 2004, he co-authored WorldatWork's newest sales compensation course, Sales Compensation for Complex Selling Models. He can be contacted at jerry@collettifiss.com.

Mary S. Fiss is a partner in the management consulting firm Colletti-Fiss, LLC. She has extensive experience in the development and implementation of team and individual compensation, reward and recognition, professional development and performance management programs. Mary works with clients on issues and challenges related to increasing sales force productivity through the effective use of compensation and management education programs.

Mary is frequently quoted in popular business publications and is the author of more than a dozen articles, book chapters and books. She and Jerry Colletti co-authored the book, *Compensating New Sales Roles: How to Design Rewards That Work in Today's Selling Environment*, published by AMACOM in May 2001. She can be contacted at mary@collettifiss.com.

Ted Briggs specializes in the development and implementation of sales management strategies and programs with particular emphasis in sales compensation design solutions. A senior consultant and the national thought leader for Watson Wyatt's Sales Management and Rewards Practice, Ted has more than 20 years of client service experience. His experience crosses many industries with nationally recognized expertise in technology and telecommunications companies, and leads an annual industry forum called the High-Tech Sales Compensation Round-Table.

Ted holds a Bachelor of Science degree in organizational behavior from The University of Southern California. He earned a master's in finance and accounting from Tulane University. He can be contacted at ted.briggs@watsonwyatt.com.

Scott Sands specializes in the alignment of sales and marketing organizations with corporate strategies, financial plans and customer preferences. A senior consultant at Watson Wyatt, Scott has 12 years of client service experience. His experience crosses many industries with nationally recognized expertise in technology, telecommunications, pharmaceutical and financial services companies.

Scott holds a Bachelor of Engineering degree in Electrical Engineering from Vanderbilt University. He earned a master's in marketing and organizational effectiveness from The University of Texas. He can be contacted at scott.sands@watsonwyatt.com.